21 and Up

THE ULTIMATE, PRACTICAL, NO-B.S. GUIDE FOR ENTERING THE WORLD OF BAR LIFE

Justin Gosnell

Copyright © 2018 by Justin Gosnell

All rights reserved. No portion of this book may be reproduced in any form without permission from the author, except as permitted by U.S. copyright law.

Cover by Erin Tyler

Content assistance by Ann Maynard

Additional editing assistance by Stephanie Hart

Layout design by Pavkov Srđan

Book images created by Justin Gosnell, with the exception of the "Bar Master Award" created by Ann Maynard

ISBN: 9781731181473

Coleman, Knowledge is Power! Happy 21st

4·23·2020

Mom

> I love reading sh*t you write; you should write a book!
>
> **Jake Bowen**

The comment that started it all. Thank you, Jake.

TABLE OF CONTENTS

Introduction: A Familiar Scene 7

CHAPTER 1:
Going Out And Getting In 15

CHAPTER 2:
What Should I Get? 23

CHAPTER 3:
The Right Way To Interact With The Bartender 47

CHAPTER 4:
Tipping! 77

CHAPTER 5:
Jesus Christ, Start A Tab! 89

CHAPTER 6:
Other Rules, Etiquette, And Tips To Improve
Your Bar Experience 103

CHAPTER 7:
Balancing Drinking And Your Health 123

CHAPTER 8:
Oh God, The Hangover! 135

CHAPTER 9:
So, You Ruined Your Night 139

CHAPTER 10:
Last Call! 145

INTRODUCTION: A FAMILIAR SCENE

It's a Saturday night, and the bar is packed six people deep. Everyone's smooshed in trying to get their light beer and shot of Fireball and, by all accounts, failing miserably at doing so. All of a sudden, and with little fanfare, you see the bartender appear to lock in and acknowledge someone way back behind you. Maybe all you see is a head nod, or a hand gesture or two. Then like a gazelle blasting across an Ethiopian plain, drinks are produced and passed over the top of the huge mass of thirsty zombies to this seemingly random dude *alllllll the way in the back*. It's a scene that's not unlike the one Michelangelo painted on the Sistine Chapel depicting God reaching out to Adam.

"That's not fair, I was here before them!" will be your first thought. "He must be the bartender's friend" will be your second. But the truth is that's probably not the case at all. So then why did that other guy get the hookup?! What does he have that you don't?

The answer is simple: he is an expert in a sea of newbs. Whether it's because he worked in the service industry, learned from someone who did, or has figured out these lessons on his own, that guy is a bar *master*. And he'll probably be half-finished with his beer before you get your order in.

Through his actions, this customer established himself as a priority in the bartender's mind— and let me tell you, once you're a priority to a bartender, you're golden. You will appear connected and important, and you won't have to wait amongst the plebes like everyone else does. Anyone you brought with you (and anyone else around you) will be impressed.

No more fighting your way to the bar each round, no more looking lost in a sea of confused half-wits, no more being an average Joe sitting at the bottom of the bar scene food chain, and most importantly: no more waiting an eternity for drinks ever again.

Well, jeez… if only there were a step-by-step how-to book out there that could tell you how to achieve this outcome for yourself. *Oh wait, there is!*

WELCOME
to the
BEST DAMN GUIDE YOU'LL EVER READ ON BECOMING AN ACE AT HITTING THE BAR SCENE.

Usually, the introduction part of the book tells about the author, their vast experience, and *blah, blah, blah*—nobody cares. I'm going to cut right through the bullshit and give it to you straight. I've been bartending for well over a decade and working in the restaurant business itself for over twenty years. From corporate chains to local hot spots, to private events, I've done every brand of bartending you can imagine. As a consumer sitting on your side of the bar, I've drunk in every kind of bar they make in almost every state in America and over 30 different countries worldwide. The biggest realization I've had is that 99.9% of you are doing it wrong. Not just a little wrong, WAY wrong. It isn't even just "Freshly 21's." Some people that frequent bars regularly into old age have never had it right, and as a result, aren't reaping the MANY rewards that come with knowing how to work the scene.

So how do you get it right?

There's no real easy answer to that question. I believe that getting it right comes from a combination of three separate areas of understanding.

THE FIRST PART
is having a basic understanding of bars and the drinks themselves from a logistical standpoint. That includes knowing the pros and cons of specific bars, knowing a bit about beer, wine, liquor, how tabs work, and so on. In other words, knowing how to act like you've been there.

THE SECOND PART
comes from an understanding of basic social etiquette. Demonstrating some social intelligence goes a long way not only in just bars and restaurants—but also in any other social situation. Knowing how to speak to people, knowing how to react to certain circumstances, knowing how to share personal space, etc. are all markers that you can capably navigate life as a non-idiot.

THE THIRD PART
comes from an understanding of what a bartender's job is and, more importantly, what they have to deal with on a nightly basis. If you can tell when a bartender is busy or not, know the right things to say to them, and how to make their job easier, they're going to recognize it immediately. And they'll probably treat you better accordingly.

It's no secret that people that have been in the restaurant business themselves have better nights out than those that haven't. That's because they get it. All of those three areas of understanding I listed above were ingrained in their brains as part of their job, so they have empathy. You'll hear people say time and time again something along the lines of this: "Every person should have to work at least one year in the restaurant business/customer service business." And they say it for a good reason: everyone would be a better social citizen. They'd *get* it.

With that last thought in mind, we've now arrived at my purpose for writing this book: I want to help you get it without ever having to work a single day of your life in the bar/restaurant industry. No experience, NO PROBLEM! This book is for YOU! I promise that if you take the time to read and retain the info that fills these pages your nights out are going to be vastly better in ways you can't even imagine yet. Think about it for a second. You spend so much time going out; why wouldn't you want to get the best benefits available and reap the most rewards possible during that time?!

So without further ado, let's take that first step into bar mastery.

BUT, FIRST...

Before getting to the "good stuff," there are two important things we have to go over.

If you're not of age to legally drink, STAY HOME!

Don't use a fake ID or an older sibling/friend's ID, E V E R !

The penalties for getting caught with a fake ID and/or drinking underage can have some severe consequences. Why start the beginning of your adult life out on a bad foot just because you couldn't wait one more year to be legal? Have some patience. Your time will be here before you know it.

It's also worth taking into consideration that using a fake ID in a bar is a very selfish act. When a problem does arise from someone either getting caught with it or from an incident occurring, it often results in an innocent person losing their job or even their business.

If you don't take this advice, and you *do* get caught with a fake ID, don't argue. Even if you get the ID taken from you, don't try to get it back; just take it as a lesson learned and leave immediately. Arguing will only result in them taking it up a notch and calling the cops. At that point, you could get charged with using false identification.

If you are of age or are just reading all of this ahead of time to be prepared for when you are legal, then GREAT! Let's then move on to my second piece of advice.

02 | If you can't afford to be out drinking at a bar, don't be out drinking at a bar.

If you walk up to the bar and ask, "What's the cheapest thing you have that's also the strongest," you may be better off just staying home and saving your money. I see credit cards get declined nightly for something as cheap as a $3 drink. Once I saw a young girl order one Bud Light, and then ask me if I could split the cost of it across THREE separate credit cards. "They'll get declined if you do the full amount," she said. The beer cost $4.25. If this is you, *stay home!*

When you're young, bars seem like this magical place where all this amazing stuff is going down— and you can't be a part of it because you can't get in. I know it's hard to believe, but the truth is that you don't need to be in a bar to have fun. Get together with a few friends, maybe all chip in on a cheap bottle of booze, and play a board game. I promise you'll have a much better night going this route, and you'll feel way better when looking at your bank account the next morning.

Now that I've gotten that out of the way and you're sure you have some funds at your disposal for a fun night out, it's time to get started.

CHAPTER 1:

GOING OUT AND GETTING IN

It was Benjamin Franklin that famously said "By failing to prepare, you are preparing to fail." That quote doesn't just apply to succeeding at work or school, doing a little preparation for something as simple as a night out can be the difference between having just an okay time versus an amazing one. Here are some basic tips to kick off your evening out.

Formulate a game plan for your evening ahead of time. Before picking a bar, decide what the purpose of your night is before you go out and plan accordingly. Just going to one place to watch a game? Great! Figure out which bar is showing the game ahead of time, bring a credit card, and run a tab! Hitting downtown and doing a bar crawl where you know you'll be bouncing from bar to bar and getting trashed? Awesome! Hit an ATM first and grab some cash so you can freely move on to the next place without the hassle of having to close out tabs.

> **PRO TIP:** *Set a budget! With credit cards, it can be easy to get carried away once the drinks are flowing and everyone's buying rounds of shots. Hitting an ATM before your night out, grabbing a set amount of cash—say $100—and limiting yourself to spending ONLY that is an easy way to keep track of the damage for the night. I suggest bringing a variety of different denominations, so paying is quick and easy and doesn't require that you wait for change from a bartender.*

If your budget is $100, bring (3) $20's, (2) $10's, (2) $5's, and (10) $1's. It's even better if you're familiar with a bar and know how much your go-to drink costs. Your budget can then also be a guideline for knowing when you've had enough for the evening. For example, if you want to limit yourself to five drinks for the night, and you know the drink you always order costs $3, and you always leave a $1 tip each round, you can bring exactly $20. Once that money is gone, you'll know it's time to call it a night. Yep, it's Budgeting 101 but way more fun because we're talking about booze!

Learn a little bit about each bar and what it offers before deciding where to go. It never ceases to amaze me the number of inexperienced people that walk into a bar and have no idea where they are or what the bar is about. Having at least some understanding of the place you're walking into is important and will ultimately save you some embarrassment. If you walk into a bar that only features microbrews on tap and try to order a draft PBR, you're going to look like a clown. Similarly, if you walk into a classy wine bar with that same order then Jesus, you might as well just put on a red nose and some face paint.

Not all bars are created equal, and the best advice I can offer you is to think of picking a bar in the same way that you would choose a restaurant. Before you go out to eat with friends, you usually decide what you're in the mood for and everyone agrees on it. Chinese? Italian? Sushi? Indian? Comfort food? You'd *hopefully* know better than to try to order a burger and fries at a hole-in-the-wall sushi joint, right? And, if you did want sushi, you wouldn't order it at a pizza spot, right?!

Choosing a bar is the same way. Maybe you're looking for some low-key conversation with friends? Loud music and dancing? Live music? Want to play some pool or darts? Want to watch a sporting event? Want a good beer? A big wine list? Fruity cocktails? Decide on that first and then start looking at which bars offer what you're in the mood to do. You don't want ever to be the guy that goes into a quiet, low-key bar, asks them to turn the one small TV to sports, and then starts freaking out with every play, chest-bumping his buddies and slamming shots and disrupting everyone else's time. They have places made specifically for that kind of behavior [Hint: it's called Buffalo Wild Wings].

PRO TIP: *Spending a few minutes checking out different bars websites is a great way to see what each one has to offer. If it's a decent bar, they'll have their entire menu online, drink specials they offer, any upcoming events they're promoting, etc.*

ALWAYS have your ID with you. Bringing a valid ID should be a no-brainer, but sadly it seems it isn't. I don't care if you're 70, you should always have it with you. Some bars card anyone who walks through the door—and if you don't have one, you're not getting inside. It sucks to be the one that kills the night for the whole group. I've seen entire parties of 20 people or more have to leave a bar because one 23-year-old didn't think she'd need her ID that night, ruining the entire evening for everyone. Trust me when I say that you do not want to be that person.

PRO TIP: *Before going out, do a quick check online to see what constitutes being a valid ID in your county/state. Typically, it is always a driver's license or ID card issued by the D.M.V./M.V.A., a passport, or a military ID. And that's it. You can always tell you're dealing with a rookie when they try to use a college ID, Social Security card, library card, credit card, a birth certificate, or a photo on their phone of their ID, etc. NONE of those are acceptable! It's also important that your ID is in good shape. If it's cracked, the lamination is worn off or peeled back, faded, etc., pony up the dough to get it replaced. It varies how strict each bar will be. Just be aware there are places that will not accept your ID if it's in rough condition.*

Be prepared. In addition to your ID, always bring a CHARGED cell phone, two credit cards, some cash, some quarters, and if you'd like, some mints/gum. I've seen entire nights get thrown off due to one of those things missing. If you get separated from your group, how will you call them if you didn't bring a phone? If the bar or club you're trying to get into is charging a cash-only cover charge, your credit card alone won't help you. Can't park at a meter because you have no quarters? Can't seal the deal because your breath smells like ass? Don't let stupid things like that put a damper on your night. Those are rookie mistakes!

PRO TIP: *Keep an emergency number written on paper in your wallet/purse/phone case/etc. If anything happens to you, or if you accidentally lose your wallet/purse, there's a far better chance someone will find it and contact you if they can easily find a number to call. Also, if you have a feature on your phone that helps you track it if it goes missing, set it up before you start barhopping. I can't tell you how many people I've heard cursing themselves after losing their phones because they'd procrastinated setting up their phones tracking software.*

Dress Codes. Like it or not, you can't wear basketball shorts and sandals everywhere. And honestly, if that's how you're trying to live your life, you're better off watching TV at home with a six-pack of Natty Light. (It's probably what you'd rather do anyway, amirite?) And while some bars might be down with your schlub-chic vibe, others won't let you across the threshold.

It's totally up to each bar to decide what they will or won't allow, and the list runs the gamut from hats to jeans, flip-flops, bandanas, offensive t-shirts, certain colors (especially in areas prone to more gang activity), baggy clothes, and chain wallets. And believe me, they're not going to be willing to "let you slide" if you stroll up decked out in off-limits gear. So if you and your friends have picked a spot for the weekend and you don't know if there's a dress code, it's worth a couple of minutes to check their website, Yelp, or even picking up the phone.

PRO TIP: *Keep an extra set of clothes in the trunk of your car. You never know when you'll need it. You could get caught in the rain, the temperature could end up dropping drastically as the sun goes down, someone could spill a drink on you or—God forbid—puke on you. You just never know.*

When it comes to organizing your group for a night out don't be afraid to step up and be the leader. Be the one that checks the websites, makes the calls, makes sure everyone has their ID's, etc. Not only does it show your friends that you care, it also shows everyone that you know what you're doing—and *nothing's* cooler than a person who knows how to handle themselves in every situation.

CHAPTER 2:

WHAT SHOULD I GET?

Choosing what you drink may just be the most important factor in how your evening ends up. It determines how fast you're going to get drunk, how many calories you're going to take in, how much trouble you'll have getting to sleep later, and most importantly, how hungover you'll be the next day.

Before I start making suggestions on how to figure out what to order, here are a few things to keep in mind.

Drinker's Math: In the United States, a standard drink contains 0.6 ounces of pure alcohol. This amount of pure alcohol is typically found in:

(1) 12 oz. beer (5% alcohol content)
(1) 8 oz. glass of malt liquor (7% alcohol content)
(1) 5 oz. glass of wine (12% alcohol content)
(1) 1.5 oz. "shot" of 80 proof liquor (vodka, gin, rum, whiskey, tequila, etc.)

Each of these drinks on average takes about one hour to process out of your system [Note: various factors can alter this processing time, such as how full your stomach is and how much water you've been ingesting].

Knowing what you're drinking will get you respect. It's simple: the more you know about your drink, the more it looks like you know what you're doing. This, in turn, earns you more respect from the bartender. I mean, after all, this is something you're putting in your body, so shouldn't you *at least* know a bit about it before you throw it down your gullet?!

If someone only tells me they want a martini, I then have to ask, "Do you want gin or vodka? What kind? Up or on the rocks? Olives? Lemon wedge? Lime twist?" If you instead said, "I'd like a Ketel One martini, slightly dirty, up, with three olives on the side and no vermouth," I *instantly* know I'm dealing with a person that knows what the hell they're doing. Just by doing something as simple as placing a drink order, this person has already made a good impression on the bartender.

This also applies to "unique" orders. If your favorite drink is kind of obscure, then you should *at least* know what goes in it. If you just walk up and say, "Do you know how to make a Sparkling Pink Flamingo shot?" you're probably going to be met with blank states. Most bartenders will have no idea what you're talking about, and if they're busy, they sure as hell won't Google it for you. However, if you know it's equal parts watermelon Pucker, Goldschläger, and cranberry juice, *just ask for that.*

> **PRO TIP:** *Don't EVER say "You're the bartender, you should know!" There are literally tens of thousands of recipes out there—maybe more—and not a single bartender in the world knows them all. If a bartender doesn't know what's in your drink, just tell them. Insulting them will get you nowhere and knowing an obscure drink recipe doesn't impress anyone.*

You Do You...But Be Aware of the Message You're Sending. I know, some of those silly drinks can be fun. Who doesn't love a forty-ounce strawberry margarita with two upside-down Coronas stuck in it or a tropical rum drink served in a light-up bucket with six straws? There's nothing wrong with ordering a wacky drink, just be aware that it is going to make you stand out. In your head, you're thinking that you're going to stand out because it looks cool, but to *experienced* drinkers, you're just going to stand out as a person that's very young and immature. Don't care what people think?! Great! I'm only pointing it out to provide awareness because this *is* a guide on how to appear cooler and more mature in the bar scene.

The "Most Expensive" Doesn't Mean It's "The Best." Yeah, I get it. You're a rich kid with your mom and dad's credit card, and they don't give a damn what you spend on it. That's great and all, but let's be clear: you can't purchase maturity or real coolness—at least, not at a bar. If you think that buying 18-year-old scotch as shots for your buddies, or even more common, for girls you're trying to impress, is going to work, you're wrong. What's even worse is that you also look like a huge douche. A 21-year-old female is not going to have fun shooting scotch, regardless of whether it's the cheap rail brand or Lagavulin 16. I've seen different douches...err...I mean dudes, try to pull this off maybe 100 times in my life, and I can honestly tell you that every single one failed *miserably*. A few rounds of Scooby Snacks, though? Now we're talkin'!

On a similar note...

You don't need top-shelf liquor in all your drinks. There's a very simple reason that so many "college bars" get away with pouring cheap plastic bottle liquor into top-shelf bottles and selling it as pricey brands: inexperienced drinkers have no idea what they're drinking. These places will gladly charge you $8 for a "Grey Goose" and cranberry instead of $5 for a rail one, while actually giving you the rail one. They're maximizing profits by taking full advantage of the inexperience of a novice drinker (i.e. YOU).

This practice isn't even limited to just the hole in the wall college bars. In 2013, there was a massive raid in New Jersey where a major restaurant chain (rhymes with P.E.Y. Schmyday's) got busted for switching out top-shelf liquor for cheap booze. Even more alarming is that the thirteen different locations that were nabbed had allegedly been doing it for over a year without any customers noticing! In addition to those thirteen "Schmyday's," sixteen other businesses were also busted in the sting—including one that had been selling rubbing alcohol mixed with caramel coloring as scotch! Crazy, right?!

Advertising and celebrities will try and make you believe that you must have whatever expensive liquor they're peddling to have a great night. The reality is that this just isn't true. I know there's the age-old argument that higher quality liquors will produce less of a hangover, and I believe there *definitely* is some truth to that. My suggestion is to find a happy medium. Smirnoff is a great vodka that costs much less than Grey Goose, and you'll never know the difference if you're drinking it mixed in fruit juices or soda or whatever. Save the top shelf stuff for when you've developed your palette and are drinking liquor straight, like in a martini, where you can actually taste it.

Corporate/Chain restaurant drinks VS "regular" bar drinks. If you're new to drinking, trying out cocktails at a corporate chain restaurant (think Red Lobster, Olive Garden, Applebee's, etc.) can be an excellent way to immerse yourself in different boozy experiences. These kinds of restaurants put a lot of thought into their recipes and making them as appealing as they can be to the broadest customer base possible. Typically this means they are often sweeter and concocted in a way that the harsh taste of alcohol is almost nonexistent.

Inexperienced drinkers will often mistake this ease of drinkability as a sign that the drink is weak, but this is usually never the case. Big chains spend big money perfecting the taste of their drinks, which means that it's very easy for novices to end up getting completely hammered without even realizing it. That holds true whether we're talking about a signature cocktail invented by the restaurant itself, or their take on a classic bar recipe.

Here's the thing though that's really important. If you've found a cocktail you love at a corporate/signature spot **typically you can only get that exact cocktail made that exact way, in that exact glass, with that exact garnish, at that exact restaurant chain.** DO NOT be the person that walks into a local dive bar and asks the bartender if they can make the Pink Cosmo with cotton candy floating in it that you had at Outback. I promise you they won't have the stuff to make it and you'll end up just looking like a fool.

> **PRO TIP:** *If you want something pretty close to a signature cocktail you've enjoyed elsewhere, make an effort to get to know at least a few of the base ingredients that go into it. These are almost always listed on the drink menu. While it's in bad taste to walk into a bar and say "Do you know how to make that pink rum drink that Ruby Tuesday has?," it is totally fine to say "Could you whip me up something tasty with light rum, some peach schnapps, and some pineapple and cranberry juice?"*

HOW TO FIND WHAT YOU LIKE

If you don't have experience trying different types of liquor out, a solid starting point for getting into the world of mixed drinks is taking something you know you like and then adding some booze to it. Vodka is a natural choice because it won't change the flavor much. Great examples of this are a Cape Codder (vodka and cranberry juice), or a Screwdriver (vodka and orange juice). These are very simple cocktails, and any bar you hit can quickly make them. It's easy to branch out from these drinks too. For example, if you like vodka and cranberry juice, try a Cosmo (short for Cosmopolitan). That's a more sophisticated cocktail you can order that takes the basic flavors of vodka and cranberry juice and adds a hint of orange and lime.

With that in mind, here are a couple of other options you can try.

MIXED DRINKS

Do you like fruit juice?

Perhaps the most common bar mixer, juice can pair with liquor exceptionally well if you pick the right blends. Vodka is king in this department as it usually pairs well with just about any kind of juice (cranberry, OJ, grapefruit, and pineapple are all highly recommended), with rum being a close second and gin being a distant third.

Drinks:

Bay Breeze: Vodka, pineapple juice, cranberry juice
Sea Breeze: Vodka, grapefruit juice, cranberry juice
Bahama Mama: Light rum, coconut rum, grenadine, orange juice, and pineapple juice
Hurricane: Light rum, dark rum, tropical juice blend

Shots:

Kamikaze: Vodka, triple sec, and lime juice. Tastes like: An equal blend of orange and lime.
Woo Woo: Vodka, peach schnapps, and cranberry juice. Tastes like: An equal blend of peach and cranberry.
Royal Flush: Whiskey, peach schnapps, raspberry liqueur, cranberry juice. Tastes like: An equal blend of peach, raspberry, and cranberry juice.
Green Tea: Whiskey, peach schnapps, and sour mix. Tastes like: Arizona green tea.

Do you like soda?

Drinks:

Vanilla vodka and Coke: Tastes just like a Vanilla Coke!
Vanilla vodka and ginger ale: Tastes just like a Cream Soda!
Dirty Shirley: Vodka, Sprite, grenadine and a cherry. Tastes just like a Shirley Temple!
Dark and Stormy: Dark rum, lime juice, and ginger beer. An awesome drink if you love the strong taste of ginger!

Basically, any flavored vodka and soda will get you pretty close to a pleasing end result. Grape vodka mixed with Sprite tastes like a delicious grape soda. Cherry vodka mixed with Coke tastes like…. yeah….you get it.

Do you like desserts?

Drinks:

Pinnacle Whipped Vodka and Root Beer: Tastes just like a root beer float!
Bailey's on the rocks: Perfect cordial for the novice that enjoys something akin to a chocolate milk.

Shots:

Chocolate Cake: Absolut Citron, Frangelico, sugar rim, lemon wedge.
Birthday Cake: Vodka, Frangelico, sugar rim, lemon wedge.
Girl Scout Cookie: Kahlua, Baileys, peppermint schnapps.

Oatmeal Cookie: Baileys, Fireball, butterscotch schnapps.

Do you like candy?

Drinks:

Amaretto Sour: Amaretto liqueur and sour mix. Tastes like a sweet and tart blend of almond and citrus.
Nuts and Berries: Hazelnut and raspberry liqueur blended with milk. Tastes like a nice creamy milk with hints of sweet nut and berry flavors.

Shots:

Sweet Tart: Southern Comfort, raspberry liqueur, and sour mix.
White Gummy Bear: Raspberry vodka, peach schnapps, sour mix, and Sprite.
Jolly Rancher: Melon liqueur, peach schnapps, sour mix, and grenadine.
Pink Starburst: Vanilla vodka, watermelon Pucker, and sour mix.

Do you like cereal?

Shots:

Cinnamon Toast Crunch: Fireball and Rumchata.
Honey Nut Cheerio: Jack Daniels honey whiskey and Rumchata.
Fruit Loop: Three Olives Fruit Loop vodka and Rumchata.
Apple Jacks: Sour apple Pucker and Rumchata.
Cocoa Puffs: Creme de Cacao liqueur and Rumchata.

WINE

A whole book could be dedicated to wine (and there are many that are). Here are a few *very* basic suggestions I can give you.

In most cases, people start out with lighter, sweeter wines and work their way to the dryer, more full-bodied wines as their tastes develop. It's also very common to start on white wines and gradually progress to reds over time.

I believe that a solid starting point for getting used to the taste of wine is to start with Sangria. Most bars will offer a red and white version, and they'll usually be comprised of a blend of wine, brandy, triple sec (orange liqueur), various juices, simple syrup (basically liquid sugar), fresh fruit, etc. Once you dig sangria you can then take the next step and try some straight up sweeter wines (Moscato, Riesling, Pinot Noir are all recommended), and then in time progressively head into more full-bodied, drier territory.

Another great idea if you'd really like to get into wine drinking is to try pairing it with food. This was the key to me personally developing an immense love of wine. I'd tried drinking it a few times in social settings and just didn't dig it. Then on my 26th birthday, I was at a nice steakhouse and thought, "You know what? I'm going to take another shot at it." I ordered a nice glass of Chianti and paired it with a beautiful medium-rare porterhouse steak and, *holy shit*, it was like being born again. It opened up a whole new world of taste to me, and wine quickly became—and almost ten years later still is—my go-to alcoholic beverage of choice.

I'm not going to go too far into wine pairing in this book. If you'd like to know more, there are a ton of amazing books and free resources you can find online. The very basic rule of thumb is to pair white wine with chicken, fish, scallops, and lighter sauces, and pair red wine with beef, lamb, burgers, pork, and hearty sauces. Again, this is extremely basic and doesn't even begin to do wine the proper justice it deserves. If any of this sounds interesting to you, I strongly suggest you do some more reading on the subject. It truly is fascinating!

BEER

Beer is extremely common and often seen as the "less dangerous and more acceptable" member of the booze family. It's pretty standard that, by the time they turn eighteen, most kids out there have at least tried a few sips of beer—oftentimes provided by a family member. Much like wine, many people start light and then progress to the heavier beers as they get older. Some very popular light beers are Miller Light, Bud Light, and Coors Light. Usually, one of these three can be found at pretty much any bar in the country.

Many rookie drinkers also get their start on what is often referred to as "bitch beer." These are beers that are crafted in a way where they don't taste like beer, but instead something that's sweeter and more accessible. Some great examples of this are Mike's Hard Lemonade, Smirnoff Ice, Not Your Father's Root Beer, etc. There's usually a lot of sugar in these kinds of beers, so you have to be careful; the hangover from too many of these can be vicious.

An easier (and less sugar-loaded) starting point is hard cider. Angry Orchard, Woodchuck, and Redd's are all common brands. The great thing about cider is that it does taste a bit like beer, which makes it a very useful tool for beginning to develop a palette for it. From there you can progress to beers that are darker, hoppier, or more complex.

> **PRO TIP:** *Find a bar that offers a sampler. This way, instead of having to test out beers by buying one full beer at a time, you can get a variety of different beers in smaller sizes all at once. Another great tool is buying variety packs at liquor stores. Many breweries will offer a twelve-pack that has a couple of bottles each of the different beers they make. If you can, find a liquor store that'll let you mix and match your own six-packs—that is even better!*

Now that you've learned a few basic things about these different types of alcohol, let's go over the proper way to order these at a bar. There are some common mistakes that rookies always seem to make, so pay close attention here.

Ordering beer. Don't just walk up and ask, "What beer do you have?" or say, "I'll just have a beer." That'd be the same as walking into a restaurant and saying, "I'll have an entree," or asking the server to rattle off the menu items one by one. Many bars have a huge selection, so expecting the bartender just to recite the entire list is ridiculous. Instead, ask if they have a "beer list." You can be even more specific and ask if they have a list of drafts or bottled beer if that's your preference. If you prefer a draft beer instead of a bottle, specify that. If you want a chilled glass with your bottled beer, ask for it when you order it.

Ordering wine. I can always tell when I'm dealing with someone that's either a rookie or just not paying attention when they do things like trying to order a glass of wine we only offer by the bottle, or when they get a glass of Chianti and ask why it's not cold. A little bit of knowledge goes a long way here.

The same rule follows as when ordering a beer: you don't want to walk up and just ask for a glass of wine. Ask for a "wine list". Be sure to pay attention to which wines they offer by the glass and which are offered only by the bottle.

Ordering liquor. This is the trickiest of the three to nail down, but after reading this section, you should have no problem coming off as a total pro!

The basic rule of thumb when ordering a mixed drink is to always start with the booze first, then the mixer. It's especially important in this day and age since there are so many different kinds of flavored liquor on the market.

Here are a few examples:

If you want vodka mixed with orange juice and Sprite, order it by saying "I'd like a vodka, with orange juice and Sprite." DO NOT say, "I'd like an orange vodka and Sprite." What you'll be getting then is just orange flavored vodka mixed with Sprite. In this case, it isn't the bartender's fault; it's yours. They made exactly what you ordered.

If you want a certain brand of liquor, order it by replacing the kind of liquor you want (e.g. vodka, rum), with the brand name (e.g. Grey Goose, Bacardi). For example, let's say you want a vodka and orange juice made with Grey Goose. Instead of ordering a "vodka and orange juice with Grey Goose," you would instead say, "I'd like a Grey Goose with orange juice." The proper name for a vodka and orange juice is a "Screwdriver," so the truly correct way to order it would actually be "I'd like a Grey Goose Screwdriver." There's no need to keep the type of liquor in the order ("Grey Goose *vodka* and orange juice"), the bartender already knows that Grey Goose is vodka.

Then there's the ultimate ROOKIE MISTAKE: Ordering something like a "Grey Goose and Vodka." Uhhh… what?! Pair this with a few of my other top favorites ("I'll have some Coke and Rums," and, "I'll have a Makers and Mark") and you have what could easily be the quickest way possible to out yourself as a newb to any bartender taking your order.

Don't order a drink by asking for it using only a partial name or lame description. If you ask for a "vodka," you're just going to get a shot of vodka. The bartender isn't psychic; they don't know that what you wanted was a "vodka and soda." Same thing with just asking for a drink with a half-assed description: "I want that blue drink." I can make ten different drinks that are blue; you have to be specific!

Know the different "tiers" of liquor. Typically these are separated into three categories, being **RAIL** (also called **WELL**), **CALL**, and **PREMIUM**. Some bars offer an option above premium, usually called something like **ULTRA PREMIUM** or **SUPER PREMIUM**. It's important to know what falls into each of these categories to avoid making common rookie mistakes.

For example, a bar may offer a happy hour special where all "RAIL drinks" are half off. A rookie will go in there and keep ordering Grey Goose and cranberry; then when they get their check they'll complain and say, "I thought there was a half-off special?!" An experienced drinker knows that Grey Goose isn't rail vodka; a rookie doesn't. The same goes if you see a deal advertised that says something basic like "$5 drink specials"—that does not mean all drinks in the bar are $5. The rule also applies to places that give out "drink tickets." They most definitely are not going to just apply to everything behind the bar. It's your job to ask which drinks the special pricing/drink tickets pertain to.

Here's a basic rundown of the different tiers of liquor:

RAIL (a.k.a. WELL): This is the cheapest liquor a place offers. Rail does not always mean bad—that's a common misunderstanding. It can range from off-brand plastic bottle garbage all the way to pretty decent spirits. It depends on the individual place as there is no universal standard for which brands fall into which category. For example, one spot I bartend at uses pretty cheap booze for their rail liquor—which is standard—but the other bar I work in uses name brands for its rail liquor (like

Bacardi, Smirnoff, and Beefeater). Just know that the term "rail" refers to whatever the lowest cost option is for that particular kind of booze and you'll be fine. If you'd like to know what brand it is, just ask!

CALL: This is a step up from rail. This area is where all the "mid-level" brands lie.

PREMIUM: In most places, this is the best, and is also referred to as **"TOP SHELF."** These will be your most expensive versions of different kinds of spirits.

ULTRA/SUPER PREMIUM: This option may be offered in a place that has a pretty nice inventory of high-end liquor.

> **PRO TIP:** *Be careful when ordering something from a premium/ultra premium category as it usually comes with a price tag to match. Even in bars with good prices, drinks in this category can easily start at $10 and quickly go up from there. It's very common for high-end places (and even some mid-level places) to have drinks or spirits that can cost upwards of $30 each or more.*
>
> *It's especially important for you to pay very close attention to prices if you're venturing off and trying different cognacs and scotches, as some of these options can be ridiculously expensive. I've seen situations where a rookie had just pointed to a cool looking bottle and said, "I want to try THAT," and then been utterly shocked when they got their bill. A bartender typically isn't going to warn*

you that something is expensive because that can be extremely offensive, as some will take it to mean that you're insinuating that they can't afford what they ordered. So, you're on your own here.

How to order a mixed liquor drink to suit your taste:

Say you really don't want to taste the alcohol at all, or on the flip side, you want a really strong drink. There are a few bar terms you should know so you can order your drink *exactly* the way you want it without sounding clueless.

For example, let's say you are ordering a rum and Coke. You could add to that order by requesting that it be either **"TALL,"** a **"DOUBLE,"** or a **"DOUBLE TALL."**

Here's what each means:

TALL: When ordering a drink "tall," you're asking for the same amount of liquor but more mixer. For example, a tall rum and Coke would be made with the same amount of rum and more Coke to fill the larger glass. The result will be a drink that'll have a less strong alcohol taste.

DOUBLE: When ordering a "double," you're asking for double the amount of booze. It'll come in the same size glass as a regular drink would, so that means you'll not only be getting double the amount of rum, you'll be getting less Coke as well. The result is a drink that tastes *really* strong.

DOUBLE TALL: When ordering a "double tall," you're asking for double the amount of booze and also more mixer as well. So that'll be the same ratio of rum and Coke; just more of both. It'll come in a bigger glass and have a flavor profile that's much closer to a regular drink. In my experience *this* is what most people that want a stronger drink are after, they just don't know how to order it correctly. They'll ask for a double, and upon first taste, they'll cringe and say, "Eww, this tastes *too* strong. Can you please add some more mixer to it??" If this is you, the "double tall" is your answer!

In case I didn't explain that well enough, here are pictures that should make it easier to understand:

Now that we've covered a few basics on deciding what to order, let's go over a few more things that are relevant to this aspect of drinking.

Prices. Costs vary wildly depending on so many different factors that I won't even begin to go into in-depth. The area you're in, the kind of bar it is, the time of day it is, what brand of liquor you order, what kind of drink you order—all of these are factors in what a drink is potentially going to cost you. It used to be a bit easier to determine a price based on what you were ordering, and from least expensive to most expensive went something like:

Beer < House Wine < Rail liquor
Call liquor < Premium liquor < Ultra Premium liquor.

As more and more premium wines and microbrews make their way into different establishments, it's hard to tell anymore. In the same bar, a rail liquor drink may be $6, but a glass of Merlot might be $14. A call drink might be $7, but a premium microbrew beer might be $9 a bottle. If you end up going to a bar where you find that it's a bit more expensive than you thought, don't complain to the bartender. They have no say in what the pricing is.

When ordering doubles, it's usually standard practice that you'll be charged for the price of the drink twice. It some cases, bars offer a special where you can, say, get a regular drink for $5 or a double for just $3 more (making the drink $8, saving you $2). These kinds of specials are particularly popular in airports.

> **PRO TIP:** *To figure out the prices of drinks at a place, check out their menu first. Some places will have drink prices listed either on the menu itself, or on separate drink lists. If they don't, even just looking at the regular menu will give you a solid idea. If entrees range from $20 to $40 on average, it's safe to assume drinks are going to be pretty expensive. If their menu is more reasonably priced, and they have burgers/sandwiches/entrees*

that range from $8 to $15 on average, it's safe to assume drinks are going to be pretty reasonably priced as well.

Don't ask for a drink menu; ask for a *specific* drink "list." It's mostly only corporate chains that have drink menus all in one book that cover every beer they have, every wine, every cocktail, or soda. The majority of other bars/restaurants (especially nice ones) will have a different list for *each* area of drinks. You can always be on the winning end if you're specific about the kind of menu you're requesting.

For example, let's say you're at a bar, you're in the mood for wine, and you have no idea what they offer. The bartender asks you what you'd like to drink and you respond with a request to see a drink menu. If it's a bar that doesn't just have one big drink menu the bartender *now* has to ask for a more specific direction from you. This is not just a big waste of time, it clearly shows that you're a rookie drinker. In contrast, if the bartender asks you what you'd like to drink and you ask to see a wine list, it *doesn't matter* if they have a separate wine list or an all encompassing book—they're just going to immediately hand you whichever is relevant to your needs without having to ask you any additional questions.

Figure out a "go-to" cocktail. Having a simple favorite that can be made at pretty much any bar you go to is an essential tool for a sophisticated drinker. Knowing your go-to works well as a first choice or, even more so, as a quick "Plan B" when they don't have the first thing you wanted to order.

For example, my go-to is a whiskey and ginger ale/sprite. What bar can't make one of those quickly?!

Don't mix a ton of different kinds of booze together. Doing so is always a recipe for disaster. If you have a few beers, a glass of wine, a couple of White Russians (or any drink with milk/cream in it), and a tequila shot, you are going to have a bad time. You know not to have a bowl of cereal, sushi, and chili for a meal, so why would you mix all different kinds of liquor together in the same manner?! Think of all that different stuff churning in your stomach….yuck! Pick a direction and stick with it, you'll thank yourself later.

Don't go overboard with sweet drinks. You'll take in a ton of extra calories and sugar, which will equate to a tough time later getting a good night's rest. Oh yeah, this usually amplifies the hangover as well. I cover all the reasons you should avoid these kinds of drinks later on in this book.

Save "Bombs" or any drink with extreme amounts of caffeine for early in the evening. These are growing in popularity. From "Vegas Bombs," to "Jager Bombs," to "Cherry Bombs," to other energy drink infused cocktails like an "Irish Trash Can," or even just a basic "Vodka Red Bull"; there's no shortage of options in this department. Don't order these late at night, especially not at last call. One of the worst things ever is when all you want to do is fall into bed and crash, but instead, you just lay there tossing and turning for hours. The room spins, you feel like ass, and then you're ruined the next day because you're physically exhausted but still have eight Red Bulls pumping through your veins. Keep the caffeine to a minimum past 9 p.m. (even that's pushing it, the earlier, the better); you'll be glad you did.

If ordering shots have your friends all agree on one shot everyone in your group will enjoy. Shots should arrive quick and be consumed quick. It's supposed to be a type of primal bonding experience, a "we're all in this together" kind of thing. It's up to the person buying the round of shots to decide what to order, but if there's something you really can't stomach it is okay to speak up. Had "that one bad tequila night" and can't touch it again? I get it; it's all good! If your friend throws up the second Jameson hits her tongue, that's something you'll want to know before you put the order in!

The other reason it's smart to confer shot choice with the group is that ordering three different kinds of shots in a single order is a dick move. This is particularly the case if each of these shots has to be made to order (by that I mean ordering a straight shot of whiskey versus ordering a shot that's built following a recipe). If this is you, then you don't understand how doing shots is supposed to work. Don't be that guy/girl! Pick ONE shot and order it for everyone.

> **PRO TIP:** *Is a shot of straight liquor a bit too strong for your taste? Order it with a **"back"**! A "back" is a little sidecar of the mixer of your choice that's perfect for chasing shots! Here are a couple of examples of the proper way to order*

them: "I'd like a shot of Bacardi Gold with a Coke back," or, "May I please have a chilled shot of 1800 Silver with an O.J. back?"

Be careful with strong drinks. Quite a few drinks are already "doubles" from the start. Some common examples of these are: a "Long Island Iced Tea," a "Long Beach Iced Tea," a "Grateful Dead," a "Blue Motorcycle," and an "Irish Trash Can." These things can pack a major punch and are popular with inexperienced drinkers. Night after night I watch the fallout that comes with a rookie downing a few of these things and, trust me, it's not a pretty sight to witness.

If you've made it this far, congratulations, you now possess all the tools necessary to make the right choice when it comes to knowing what to order and why to order it. Now, if you could *just* get that bartenders attention...

CHAPTER 3:

THE RIGHT WAY TO INTERACT WITH THE BARTENDER

So you've found the bar you want and you know what you want to drink, now let's get in there and get some cold ones!

One of the best ways to have a good bar experience is to be the customer that knows how to order a drink. This is especially true when it's packed wall-to-wall with assholes that have no idea what they're doing. If we see you as a disorganized mess, we *will* avoid dealing with you at all costs. On the flip side, if you're kind and organized we will love you, and there's nothing better than having a bartender love you. You'll stand out like a golden lighthouse in a sea of turds!

Here's the best way to do it:

Have your ID ready. You're barely 21 and look young as hell. Prepare to get asked for your ID *a lot*. It doesn't matter if you were already carded at the door, if you already showed your ID to a different bartender when you ordered the last round, or if the same bartender already carded you the last time you were here six months ago. Keep it handy.

Have your order ready. This is a key step to staying on top of your bar game: have your order ready to go *before* the bartender comes your way.

It happens time and time again. I'll see someone flagging me down with a look of urgency, but when I ask what they'd like I get a deer in the headlights look and a stammering "oh, I don't know what I want." Seriously?! What an ass! Have your order ready to go! This rule applies whether you're ordering one drink for yourself or ten drinks for all your buddies.

Don't be the person that orders two beers, then tacks on an "oh yeah, can I also get a Bay Breeze?" once the beers are set in front of him, THEN adds, "Oh, I also need three shots of Fireball," and closes with, "Oh, damn, can you actually make that four shots?" The odds of that guy getting attention next time are slim to none.

The general rule of thumb here is that the more specific you are, the better. Want your shot of whiskey chilled or a cold glass with your bottled beer? Or perhaps a specific garnish, like salt and lime with your tequila shots (ask for them "dressed")? No problem! Just ask *when* you're ordering, not once it's arrived.

> **PRO TIP:** *To show that you really know what you're doing, put the drinks in order when talking to the bartender. It's almost always best to start out with liquor/mixed drinks, then wines, then beers—a system based on prep time. Mixed drinks always take the most time to make; wine takes no time at all to pour, and beer comes last because you'll want it to have a nice head on it when it gets set in front of you.*

Get the bartender's attention. To do this DO NOT start waving, yelling, whistling, waving money, tapping on the bar, snapping fingers, etc. If you know the bartender's name, don't yell that either! And please, please, don't yell any "buddy names" at the bartender either (i.e. chief, bro, dog, homie, homeboy, dude, guy, bartender, etc.). If you see they're already helping another customer, don't interrupt them. If they haven't acknowledged that they're taking your order yet, don't just start yelling out your order when they're close. I also strongly suggest that you not throw anything at the bartender to get their attention, and don't ever grab/touch the bartender. These are all fast ways to get thrown out of a bar.

In contrast, don't be too passive either. If you're staring at the ground, we might not know that you need anything from us. Try to make eye contact, smile, have your money out, look like you're ready to order, and wait your turn. Raising your hand is also okay. A bartender will know the signs. If you can see that they're busy and you've been waiting a bit, it is totally acceptable to say something to get their attention. The proper way to do this is to make direct eye contact and say something along the lines of, "Hey, I can see you're super slammed right now. When you get a second, could I please order a drink? I'll be standing right here."

> **PRO TIP:** *Don't make eye contact with the bartender if you don't need anything. It's awkward and frustrating for us if we catch a customer staring, walk over and ask what they need, and get told, "Oh, nothing." At the same time, it can also end up being frustrating for you if the next time we catch you making eye contact, we presume that you're just staring again and don't need anything.*

Once you have the bartender's attention, don't ask stupid questions or waste their time, especially if you can see they're very busy. Seriously, if you ask me "what's good" or "what do you have?" or say "surprise me," I immediately know you're a rookie that has no idea what they're doing. Every person has a different opinion of what's good, and without knowing you I have *no idea* what you like. Something I love might be disgusting to you!

If you instead asked, "What's something good if I like mango and pineapple?" or, "What beer do you think would be good if I love Blue Moon?" *Now* I can quickly offer a suitable suggestion for you. Don't be shy either.

Give the bartender some space. Getting in their face and screaming your order isn't cool, okay? Back up a few inches, calm down, speak loudly and clearly, and don't freak out—we've got you covered.

> **PRO TIP:** *Being polite can go a long way with a server or bartender. It should have been ingrained in you by the people that raised you, but if it wasn't I'll give you a tip: Use the words "please" and "thank you" and life will go much smoother for you.*

Pay attention to what the bartender is saying to you. Here's just one example of the *many* redundant conversations that take place time and time again:

Me: Hi, what can I get for you?

Young Customer: I'll take a Yuengling draft!

Me: I'm sorry, we don't have Yuengling. We're a microbrewery, and everything we have on tap is our beer. We do offer Bud, Bud Light, and Corona by the bottle, but everything else we have is ours.

Young Customer: Oh ok, I'll just have a Miller Light then.

Me: We don't have Miller Light. *[Repeats previous spiel.]*

Young Customer: Oh, okay. Do you have Blue Moon?

Me: *[Long sigh.]*

It *should not* take that many steps to get answers out of you. Put down your phone, stop talking to your friends, and pay attention to what's going on and what we're saying. It's our *job* to give you good information and help you have a great experience throughout your visit, but that does no good if you don't *listen*.

Don't place the same order with multiple bartenders. If you've placed an order with a bartender and they walked away, 99.9% of the time that means they're going to make your order. It may take a minute, especially if the bar is busy. Your order could be fifth in line for all the orders they just took at once. They may have needed to run and grab another bottle of liquor for your order or gone to change a keg that just blew. Have a bit of patience.

If a different bartender walks up after you placed your order, DO NOT order from them too. Just say, "Thanks, but another bartender already took my order." This happens time and time again. A customer only wanted two Vodka Cranberries, but because they were impatient, they now have three bartenders arriving at the same time with a total of six drinks. Don't be that person. **Some bars may even make you pay for all of the drinks**

that were made. If it does seem like it's taking way too long to get your drinks, then it's fine to inquire with another bartender, but let them know the situation. "Excuse me, I already ordered two Vodka Cranberries from another bartender, but it has been a long time, and I still haven't gotten them." They'll figure out what's going on and fix it accordingly.

> **PRO TIP:** *Learning a little bit about what you're drinking and where you're drinking is especially important when it comes to understanding how long you should be waiting for your drink to arrive. Think of it like food. You know that if you order a cup of soup, it will probably come out much faster than if you order a well-done steak. The same applies to different drinks.*
>
> *A bottled beer can be popped open and set on a bar in mere seconds. However, if you order a drink that requires a lot of time and effort to make—like a Mojito or an Old Fashioned—have some patience! Keep this in mind as well if you're ordering something "special." One of the bars I work at doesn't usually sell Mojitos. We probably make about five a year. We do have the ingredients (and I'm more than happy to make one for you), but it does require me to make a two-minute trip just to locate some fresh mint to use for the drink.*
>
> *Keep this kind of thing in mind when you're wondering why your two Old Fashioneds, three blackberry mojitos, two frozen*

daiquiris, and Chocolate Cake shot haven't arrived in 45 seconds. To expedite your service, don't order labor-intensive drinks when the bar is busy!

Don't walk away or relocate! This is a big one. After you've ordered your drink(s), stay right where you are! Don't waste the bartender's time by making them have to track you down. In addition to that, if you walk away after paying cash and forget your change, it by default becomes the bartender's tip. If you want your change back then stay and wait for it. It's never okay to come back twenty minutes later and say, "I forgot my change earlier, can I have it back now please?" We've already done thirty new transactions since then—how can we remember how much your change was supposed to be? Or, more acutely, why in the world would we take your drunk-ass word for it?!

Have your payment ready. Drinks cost money. I'm pretty sure this is true at all bars unless I'm missing something. With that said, I've never been able to grasp why someone looks surprised after they order a beer and I bring it and say, "Okay, that'll be $2.75." They get this look of shock on their face and then start fumbling through their pockets or purse or turn around to try to find their friend since they don't have any money on them. Really?! You're surprised you have to pay for your drink?! If you're paying cash, have it on hand when you order. If you're paying with a credit card, have it ready and…

START A TAB! Pay close attention here, because this may just be *the BIGGEST mistake rookies make.*

Nothing screams amateur more than ordering one drink at a time and proceeding to pay out on a credit card with each order. This step is so important, it has its own chapter. We'll be getting to it shortly.

Separate checks. Okay, so you want to keep your tabs separate—that's totally fine! Tell your bartender or server this BEFORE you order. Many rookies make the mistake of just assuming a bartender in a busy bar is keeping track of every single separate thing each person in your group is ordering and cataloging it accordingly. Then, at the end, after countless drinks, shots, and snacks, someone in the group will no doubt shove a credit card in my face and say, "Can I just pay for what *I* had?" Yeah, right.

Let me tell you a little secret: When a group of "friends" on a tight financial budget get one big tab at the end, it's very common for one of those "friends" to all of a sudden proclaim, "Ohhh, well only two of those drinks were mine," (nope, they had six) or, "Oooh, I thought *you* were gonna get that round of shots. It was *your* idea." NEVER in my history of bartending have I heard a person say, "I think eight of those were mine," when they only had three. It only works one way. Prevent this headache for yourself, your friends, and the bartender by being very clear about which round is going on which tab if your intention is to keep them separate.

PRO TIP: *If you didn't specify that you wanted separate checks beforehand then make it as easy as possible for the bartender to sort it out. There are a few ways to do this, the best being to just ask for a pen and mark what each person had on the receipt. Even better, if you're giving a bartender four different credit cards to run, make a note of what to charge on each tab, identifying each card using the last four digits of its number or the last name on the card. For example, just write:*

Charge $45.25 on 4675,
$45.25 on 9465,
$20.50 on 9357,
and $20.50 on 0023.

That makes it super easy and efficient! Don't ever just stuff five credit cards and a wad of cash into the checkbook and assume that we'll know exactly how you want it sorted. All this does is waste time, as we now have to make a trip back to you to ask how you want each payment processed.

Tip accordingly. It should be obvious that the way you tip has *great* influence over the way you're treated at a bar, especially if you're looking for high-end service. This must not be the case, though, because night after night I watch rookie after rookie stiff the bar on *every single round*, then watch as they act *completely dumbfounded* when trying to figure out why it's so hard for them to get more drinks. Tipping your bartender is **serious business**, so much so that I've dedicated an *entire* chapter to the subject.

Now that I've covered the basics on how to get the bartender's attention and order your drink, here's a few more quick tips that I believe are relevant to this chapter. I go into complete coverage of all bar etiquette later in the book, but for now here are a few things to keep in mind:

Once you have your drink *don't* just stand there at the bar. After you've placed your order, step aside and let others reach the bar so they can order too! It's also always a very good idea to stay clear of any path you see customers/employees using to navigate the area you're in (this especially includes doorways and hallways).

Don't stand in the service bar area! What the hell is the service bar area you ask? It's a spot where the bartender places all the drinks they've made that are awaiting pickup from cocktail waiters/servers. You can usually tell this area because, shockingly, there'll be servers there picking up drinks with tickets on them. Usually, this area has bar mats placed down, a garnish tray close by, along with straws, napkins, and other supplies. DON'T STAND HERE! You're blocking the entire bar/restaurant from getting their drinks. I've even seen people try to move chairs to this area and sit down… Don't be that guy/girl!

Don't place your empty glasses on the bar mats. Bar mats (those flat rubber things located around the bar) are where drinks are made, not where empty glasses go. It's totally okay to leave your empties just sitting right on the bar, but putting them on the mats is the equivalent of putting them on our desk. Keeping dirty glasses off the mats isn't just to help keep things organized either; it's also to keep work areas clean and free of germs.

PRO TIP: *If a bartender is making your drinks on a bar mat, don't reach out and just grab them. This happens quite often, and people end up grabbing drinks that aren't finished being made yet—or, even worse, they grab drinks that aren't even theirs. Once your drink is ready, your bartender will set it on the bar in front of you or hand it directly to you.*

Trade off buying rounds with your friends. This is typically how adults drink. If four adult friends walk in together, usually one person will pick up the first round and then the next friend will get the second, and so on. Regardless of whether you stay in one bar all night or are bouncing around bar hopping, this technique works well. It consolidates the entire payment and process down to one fast transaction and shows that you're not petty.

PRO TIP: *Don't ever be the person that starts arguing with their friend that the drink they ordered in the round that you're paying for costs 25 cents more than the drink you ordered when they were buying. You're just embarrassing yourself.*

Leave the barback alone! Busy bars usually have a barback working. There are a few different ways to spot the barback: usually, they're younger (but not always), most of the time they'll have a different uniform on, and—here's the big one—if you pay attention, you'll notice they aren't serving any customers or making any drinks! They're probably clearing dishes, stocking glasses, wiping down counters, and refilling the ice well. Don't ask them for drinks, don't ask them to close your tab, and don't ask them to get a bartender for you. That's not their job.

Conversing with the bartender. Be mindful of your surroundings. If it's slow and you can see the bar isn't too busy then, by all means, strike up a conversation! Bartenders love to give recommendations on drinks, other good hot spots in the area, or upcoming events that have something unique going on. But if the bar is slammed, and you can clearly see the bartender is doing a million things at once, this is not the time to say, "So, are you originally from this area?" or any other pointless comment or question. Keep in mind that bartenders are there to provide you with drinks, food, and service; they're not there to entertain you or keep you company if you're bored.

Telling the bartender which people need drinks. Don't *ever* do this. Wondering what I'm talking about? Let me explain.

There's always "that guy" who likes to sit at the bar and, even though he has a drink, wants to play as the bar watchdog. This guy will flail his arms and flag the bartender down just to say, "The guy behind me needs a beer!" Maybe he's trying to be helpful; maybe he's trying to play the hero for some friendly attention. Let me put a myth to rest here: you are not a "hero" if you do this.

Trust me. We can clearly see that the guy next to you needs a drink. When the bar's slammed, *everyone* needs a drink. We have an order we're working in to serve customers as quickly as possible, an order that may make no sense to you because—let's be honest here—you have no idea how to bartend. There are so many things going on that you're completely unaware of, and it could very well be the case that we are intentionally not serving a person for reasons known only to our management and us.

Contrary to popular belief, bartending is not just handing people drinks. It's also making sure people are consuming at a safe rate. It is our job not to over serve people, and we have to spend a lot of time training for that facet of our role. That guy you've never met, the one you think I'm just oblivious to and ignoring might be eight drinks deep into the evening and someone that's a known problem causer. He's being served drinks at a very deliberate pace to ensure the safety of himself and those around him. There's no way for you to know that, so the smarter play is to stay uninvolved.

Never put coasters or bar napkins in front of you. I'll let you in on a little inside bar knowledge: When more than one bartender is working, we use a silent system (usually referred to as either "flagging" or "tagging") to let the other bartenders know we've greeted a new customer. We do it by placing either a coaster or a cocktail napkin in front of them. So when you sit down and reach over and put two napkins in front of you, you've silently told all of the bartenders that you've already had your order taken. Maybe it's not a coaster or a napkin. I've been to bars where they use small side plates or rolls of silverware to mark who has been greeted.

With that thought in mind, you'll never go wrong if you always follow this rule:

Don't reach over the bar and/or touch/take/steal anything. I'm always surprised at how many people commit this offense. There is never a time when it's okay to reach over the bar and take anything. This includes playing with coasters, straws, or toothpicks, adding ice to your drink, stealing the glass your drink came in, stealing fruit from the garnish tray, grabbing the soda gun to top your drink off, trying to pour your own beer, or grabbing a liquor bottle. Also, don't ever go behind the bar. Everything I've just outlined above is a fast track to getting thrown out of a bar. If you need something just ask a bartender for it, that's what we're there for.

Be mindful of how much space you're taking up. This is especially important as the bar gets busy. Don't come in on a busy Saturday night and think it's totally cool to open up your laptop, spread out all your paperwork and books, and do homework at the bar. That may be alright if it's a slow weekday lunch and you can see that other people aren't in need of the extra spots you're taking up at a bar, but it's never okay when the bar is slammed. Coffee shops and libraries exist for a reason.

Don't ask for strong drinks unless you're willing to pay for the additional booze. It's one of the most obvious signs of a cheapskate. Every bar has a standard pour count for each cocktail/recipe. Asking someone for a strong drink is the same as asking them to steal. Would you go to a restaurant and ask for extra steak and expect it to be free?

Of course not! So why do you think asking for free alcohol is okay?

I don't care what kind of trick you think will work, we've seen and heard it all. What "tricks" am I referring to? Here are a few popular ones:

Asking for less ice: This isn't going to get you more liquor. Your drink will either come with less ice and more mixer, or it won't be filled to the top of the glass due to the ice not being there.

[NOTE: For what it's worth, "standard" drinks are *supposed* to be packed with ice. The bartender's not trying to rip you off; what's happening is a technique called "mounding." When a standard mixed drink is being made properly, you'll at first see that the ice goes so far over the top of the glass that it creates a mound. Once the liquor is added though you'll see that the ice quickly melts down. This is due to both the temperature of the alcohol (which is almost always room temperature) as well as basic thermodynamics. The higher proof the alcohol is, the faster it will melt your ice. This melt is built into the drink's recipe because that little bit of water helps take the bite out of the taste.]

Asking for just a splash of mixer: Your drink will have the same amount of alcohol, with just a splash of the mixer—meaning the drink won't be filled to the top of the glass or it'll just come in a smaller glass.

Asking for a bigger glass: Unless you asked for a "double tall" and are paying for the extra booze, you'll just be getting more mixer.

Buddying Up: Saying anything like, "Don't be shy," "Hook it up, bro," "Make it good," "Make it strong," or, "More booze than mixer," isn't going to work. Just *don't*.

> **PRO TIP:** *If you want a strong drink, the way to get this is to ask for a "double," or a "double tall." Yes, it'll cost you more, but that's life.*

Drink prices are not open to negotiation. Drink prices are set by the owner of the establishment, not the bartenders. So, no negotiating. Asking if you can get a drink that's normally $8 for $5 will get you nowhere. No pity party. Ordering something you know you can't afford only to say, "Oh damn, I'm a few cents short, can I still have it?" is going to get you a big ol' NOPE. No bribery. Asking, "Hey if I order five beers and give you a tip can I have 3 for free?" is not okay. And no bartering. No, you can't give me some weed or show me your boobs for five shots of Fireball. If you can't afford to pay for it (and by pay for it I mean with money), go to a cheaper bar or stay home.

Complaining that your drink is too weak. There could be many reasons why your drink tastes weak. It's a proven fact that the more you drink throughout the night, the less you can taste the actual alcohol. Maybe it sat there getting watered down for a while before you took your first sip. Maybe you ordered a drink where the taste of alcohol is supposed to be covered up. The truth is that the most common reason someone says their drink is too weak is because they're just lying to get free alcohol.

But what if your drink really *is* weak? This could be happening because you're acting up and the bartenders are trying to scale down your intake. It could also be happening because you've just been an absolute jerk to deal with, or you have been stiffing the bartender each round.

If your drink tastes different than it does at a different bar. This is totally normal. There are thousands upon thousands of recipes out there for different cocktails, and there is not a single bartender in the world that knows them all. Even "standard" drinks have multiple variations on recipes. If you ever go to a bookstore or online to check recipes, you'll notice how often this is the case. A little variation from bar to bar—or even bartender to bartender—is par for the course.

> **PRO TIP:** *If you do know a recipe or two, don't be the person that shouts, "You're making that wrong," or, "That's not what it says online," or, "ACTUALLY, they do it a different way across the street." Nothing good will come out of that kind of behavior.*

If your drink gets spilled or knocked over. If you spilled it by being careless, it's your fault, and you should just suck it up and buy another one. If someone else bumped into you and spilled it, that's their fault, and they should offer you another one. Some bars can be pretty cool when it comes to replacing things when accidents happen (the key word being *accidents*). Don't abuse their kindness. If you were acting like an out of control ass and it cost you your drink, you may just be on your own here.

If you sent someone else to get your drink and it's wrong, too bad. Seriously. If you were too lazy to go up and get it yourself, don't come bitching at the bartender when your buddy gets your order wrong, and certainly don't demand it get replaced for free. If your drink meant that much to you, then you should have just come up and ordered it yourself.

If you're ordering a bunch of drinks, have somebody help you carry them. Don't ask for a tray, and certainly don't ask a busy bartender to come around the bar and do it.

Don't assume every bartender knows what you're drinking. If you want three more rum and Cokes, then ask for that. If you walk up to a bartender and just say "I want three more of these" while holding your empty glasses with a bit of ice and an old lime left in them, they'll probably have no idea what you need. This is especially true if you're not a regular, or if it's a very busy bar, or if it's not even the same bartender that took your first order.

Respect the end of happy hour. It's completely okay to ask if you can get one more in before happy hour ends in five minutes. It's NOT okay to ask if you can be rung up for eight more drinks before Happy Hour ends. It's also not ok to flag down the bartender two minutes past the time when a drink deal ends, asking if you can get one more drink rung in at the special price. If you do happen to do this and the bartender says that they can't honor the request, respect it.

This scenario happens a lot, and when I tell people there's nothing I can do, they get angry and take it out on me. They think I have the ability to hook them up with the special pricing and that I'm just not doing it out of spite or something. The truth is that our computer systems update automatically at the set times for when a drink special begins and ends. If the special runs from 4:00 p.m. to 7:00 p.m. there's a button that says "Happy Hour Beer" that rings up for the special price. At 7:01 p.m. that button doesn't exist anymore, and there's no "trick" I can do to make it reappear.

Don't order water "for everyone." Let me be specific about what I'm referring to here. A guy comes in with a group of ten other people, comes up to the bar, asks for water, and then says, "You know what? How about we just get a water for everyone?" This always plays out the same way. I then waste time making eleven glasses of water and placing them on the bar. The guy that ordered them drinks most of his; one or two other people have a sip of theirs, then the other eight are left untouched only to end up getting poured out once the pack moves on to the next bar. It's a total waste of time, water, and plastic (if a plastic cup is used or there's a straw in it). This waste is especially bad if you're in an area that's conserving water. Your friends are big boys/girls. If they want some H2O, they can ask for it.

Don't make fun of what someone else is drinking. This just makes you look like an insecure jerk, a bully, or an "alpha bro." Guys try to show off in front of girls or their other friends by doing this all the time, and they always end up looking like assholes, especially when they keep harping on it and won't let it go. The truth is that nine times out of ten there's no real logic behind it. I'll watch some guy drinking a Budweiser endlessly berate a "friend" because he's chosen to drink a Cosmo, even though the Cosmo is actually twice as strong as a Budweiser. Don't do that. People like what they like and should be free to drink what they want to drink.

Don't be a "post-shot show-off." I get it, you just slammed an "Irish Car Bomb" like a champ—*congratulations*. I hate to be the one to tell you this, but *nobody cares*. When you slam your glass on the bar, it doesn't make you look tougher, or like some boozing badass; it makes you look like a massive douche that's trying way too hard to draw attention to yourself. For guys out there, the "post-shot show-off no-no's" also include grunting, yelling either "WHHHHEEEWWWW," or "F%&K YEAAHHHHH," and for girls this includes yelling "WOOOOOOO," "YEAAHHHHH," or just screeching in general.

Don't make out in front of the bartender. Seriously, we don't want to see that shit, and neither does anyone else. It is especially annoying if we're trying to talk to you about your order or close your tab, and can't get your attention. Stop sucking face long enough to let us do our job.

If you see the bartender mess up a drink. DO NOT call out and ask to have it for free. It's totally up to them where that drink goes, and I can assure you that in most cases it *never* ends up going to the person that blatantly asks for it.

If you're not digging the way a particular bartender is treating you, go to a different one. You don't always have to go to the same person; there are different people working for a reason! With that said, if you feel like the bartender is being rude to you, don't argue with them, just walk away and speak to a manager.

Be wary of who you're accepting drinks from. Ladies, this is directed at you. I see it all the time with girls new to the bar scene. They make the mistake of just accepting random drinks from anyone who buys them. Of course, there's the issue of roofies (which we'll get to in a second), but even aside from that, there's the issue of having to at some point deal with the person that's been buying all those drinks for you.

Let's be realistic here. If a guy is buying you drinks it's because he's interested in you—or more specifically, he wants something from you. It could be just some company/small talk, it could be a potential date, or it could be sex. Of course, you don't owe anyone anything if they buy you a drink. But that fact alone won't stop them from at least trying to interact/approach you in some way at some point in the evening.

The bottom line is: If you don't have any interest at all in the guy then you shouldn't accept drinks from him all night. Knowing how to prevent those kinds of situations from happening will save you from a ton of awkward situations later on. If someone sends you a drink and you're not interested, send it back. If someone at the bar offers to pay for your drink and you're not interested, say "no, thank you." It's better to stay safe than it is to score a free drink.

Watch your drink. ALWAYS. Girls, again, this is especially important for you. It's unfortunate, but roofies (slang for date rape drugs) are a thing. Never turn your back on your drink, and if you head to the bathroom either have a trusted friend keep an eye on it for you or take it with you. If someone buys you a drink make sure you see it come directly from a bartender. DO NOT accept anything someone randomly hands to you. If you ever start to feel woozy, out of it, like you're sedated, or anything like that, seek help immediately.

Keep an eye on all personal belongings. Here is something many novices overlook while out drinking. It's not the bartender's job to watch your stuff while you're mingling around the bar, dancing, going outside to smoke, making a phone call, whatever—it's YOURS. It's especially not the bartender's job to store your stuff, so don't even ask. You're in a public area, which in turn means that you're surrounded by people of all types, with all kinds of different morals/values/motives. With that said, don't leave your purse, wallet, smartphone, etc., just sitting out in the open. Consolidate what you're taking with you on your night out as much as possible. Try wearing pants with deep pockets, or if you're a girl, carry the smallest purse possible. Don't keep all your cash on you—just take what you'll need for the night.

PRO TIP: *If you already own a smartphone, purchase a case for it that has a couple built-in slots for storing a few small belongings. Then you'll have your phone, your ID, a credit card or two, and some cash all in one easy to protect package. If your pants have pockets with either a zipper, buttons, or Velcro, even better!*

Don't take your shoes off. Girls, this is especially directed at you. I can't even begin to tell you how gross a bar floor looks when the lights come up after a night of heavy traffic. Not only that, there's a very likely possibility that there are remnants of broken glass somewhere on the floor. With that in mind, I strongly suggest that you keep your shoes on at all times. In most areas it's not just a rule, it's the law.

Don't leave any money sitting out on the bar unless you're leaving it for a tip. A bar top is a place reserved for money that's being left to either cover a tab or tip. Seriously, if your cash is not intended to be left for either of those purposes, then put it back in your wallet/purse. If you leave your money just sitting out on the bar and it ends up in the bartender's tip jar, or worse, in someone else's pocket, it's your fault.

Don't steal the bartenders' tips. Sad I even have to say this. If you see a tip jar, do not stick your hand in it and take the money. More commonly, if you see cash left on the bar by a previous customer, do not steal it. Do I really have to tell you that's not okay?!

If you want to get rid of your gum. Just ask the bartender for a napkin if you don't see any placed around the bar area, then put it in the napkin and toss it in the trash. Please don't just stick it under the bar/table, on your food plate, in your empty glass, in your cloth napkin, on the menu, etc. You're not five years old anymore.

If you spill a drink, tell a bartender. It happens all the time, and we have the tools and the know-how to get it cleaned up in a flash. Don't hide it from us, don't grab gobs of napkins and waste them, don't place menus over it, just fess up to it and we'll be far more appreciative. If it's a drink that has hit the floor, it becomes an even bigger safety issue, and we have to get a mop there immediately so it gets cleaned up and dries as fast as it possibly can.

Never put your head down on the bar or at a table. This is the universal sign that it's time for you to be cut off. Don't be surprised when it happens.

If someone says you're slurring or that you're too loud, take it down a notch. Don't be that person in denial. They're more than likely saying it because they're looking out for you (or because you're embarrassing yourself). So, if you ever hear someone drop that line on you, slow down on the booze a bit, have some water, and regroup.

Pace yourself and don't get too wasted. Don't be the rookie that always pukes, passes out on the bar, has to be carried out, or loses all their belongings. Getting too wasted may just be the biggest mistake a novice drinker can make, so trust me when I say that not overdoing it is essential to you having a good night.

The raw truth is that the person that's always a complete shit show by 5:00 p.m. just looks like a total ass. Your friends don't want to deal with it, the people around you don't want to deal with it, and the bartenders sure as hell don't want to deal with it either. In addition to that, you without a doubt aren't going to want to deal with the hangover that's coming the next day, either.

> **PRO TIP:** *In addition to trying to consume at least one glass of water with every alcoholic beverage you have, also try to keep a tally going of how many drinks you've had throughout the night. There are a couple of ways to do this. Putting tally marks on your arm with a pen or keeping the straw from each drink sitting next to your coaster are good ones. If the drinks are being served in plastic cups, placing each new drink you get into an ever-growing stack that you hold in your hand also works. It doesn't matter how you keep track, just make sure that you do. Drinks take time to hit you, especially when we're talking about shots, so keep track and be careful.*

If you get cut off DO NOT try to order more drinks. If your buddy is cut off, DO NOT try to order an extra drink and give it to them. If you do this, you'll more than likely be cut off, and possibly tossed out.

Don't argue with the bartender/manager. If they ask you to stop doing something, stop it. If they tell you it's time to leave, do it. Arguing never works; it just makes you look bad to everyone else around you. If they've asked you to either stop doing something or to leave, the chances are that you've done something to warrant this. Even if you feel that it's just a misunderstanding, the best idea is to leave and come back at a different time for a fresh start.

If you're going to puke. For the love of God, PLEASE go to the bathroom and get it in a toilet. You're by now at least 21 years old; you should know the telltale signs your body gives when you're about to yak. Puking on the bar, the floor, the tables, other people, etc. is never okay. If you can't make it to the bathroom, at least get it in a trashcan.

Once the lights are up, and last call is done, it's over! Don't be the guy that keeps begging to get drinks after the lights are up and the music is off. The bar is closed. It's time to move on, buddy!

DO NOT drive after you've been drinking. Yes, you've heard this before a million times, but yet you still don't listen. Why? Because you're young and invincible and think that it can't happen to you. Sadly, you won't realize that it can until it's too late. Even if you don't end up killing yourself, your friends, or an innocent family, just getting a DUI itself is serious business. States are cracking down, and you could end up with huge fines, jail time, and your license getting revoked. In Maryland (where I currently reside), if you're under 21 and weigh 160 lbs. or less, having one beer is enough to get a DUI, and if you're over 21 and under 200 lbs. having one Long Island Iced Tea is enough. It's no joke. Why start your adult life out with that already stacked against you?! With so many options available, from taxis to Uber, or parents or friends willing to help, there's absolutely no reason why you should be driving drunk.

> **PRO TIP:** *If you know you're going to be getting wrecked for the night, find a safe place to leave your car BEFORE that happens. Working downtown, I see it all the time. Someone's out drinking and decides to take a cab home. Good for them! The problem is that they left their car in a parking spot that was safe from 5:00 p.m. until 7 a.m. so now it's been sitting in that same space all afternoon and is covered with tickets—or even worse, it got towed. ALWAYS check signs/rules for where you park regardless if it's a metered spot, parking garage, or resident space.*

You might get a D.U.I. even if you're not driving a car. Yes, this is true. Depending on where you live, it is possible to get a D.U.I. from operating anything that has wheels. That could mean a bicycle, a skateboard, a lawnmower, a scooter, skates—literally *anything*. One of my good buddies thought he was safe getting home because he was riding a mountain bike. After getting pulled over and getting a D.U.I., he learned the hard way that his assumption was wrong. I strongly suggest you check what the local laws are in your area and abide by them. And when in doubt, call a cab or an Uber.

Out of all the tips in this chapter, if there's anything that sticks with you after reading it I really hope it's how important your own safety is. I can't stress enough how quickly things can go south when irresponsible decisions are made on what was supposed to just be a fun night out with friends.

CHAPTER 4:

TIPPING!

It's time to tackle the topic of tipping.

You can debate all day whether tipping should or should not be a thing, and you are completely entitled to your beliefs. I'm not even going to begin to get into that in this book. Just understand that until a change does occur in the industry in America (or I should say, if), this is how it works. Bartenders and servers make their living off of tips, so stiffing your bartender is entirely unacceptable.

The sheer amount of people that do this and then can't understand why they have a hard time getting the bartender's attention for their next order never ceases to amaze me. Not only is this how it works as a standard, but tipping also one of the key ways to take your bar experience to the next level, which is what this book is all about. I will tell you flat out: if you're a shitty tipper (or God forbid a non-tipper), you will never be in good graces with the staff at any bar you frequent. You will never get priority treatment. It's that simple.

If you're a bad or non-tipper and you're dealing with professional bartenders, they won't be rude to you. They'll just provide you with the absolute bare minimum of service required. Typically this minimum service will come after all of the other customers that are tipping correctly have been taken care of. If they're not professional bartenders, well, they may just completely ignore you, or if they do decide to serve you, they'll give you a drink that's weak as hell.

It doesn't have to be extravagant. I'm not going to sit here and tell you the only way to have a great night at a bar is to throw down a $20 tip on every

$10 round–that's not the case at all. In most bars, drinks are priced so that just leaving a buck or two is enough to constitute a good tip.

Follow these general guidelines, and you'll be good to go:

20% is the standard for a good tip. It's easy to figure out what 20% is by just dividing the cost of your tab by five. If the drink's $5, then the tip should be at least $1. If the drink's $10, the tip should be at least $2. If the entire round you bought was $25, then the tip should be at least $5. If the whole tab for the night was $100, then the tip should be at least $20. Easy, right?

Never tip less than $1 on a drink. The 20% rule *only* applies to tabs that start at $5 and go up from there. For anything less than $5 throw down $1. So, if the drink is $2.50, leave a $1 tip. If the drink is $4, leave a $1 tip.

> **PRO TIP:** *This is especially important to keep in mind during any hours that a bar has drink specials/happy hour. A lot of cheapskates come out for those kinds of events, and tip horribly–or don't tip at all. If you're giving at least $1 tip on each drink, it's a great way to get on the good side of your bartender, so you get your drinks faster than everyone else.*

If leaving a cash tip, leave it "as is" and out in plain sight. Sometimes people try to do 'cool' things like fold it into an origami crane, or into a mini origami t-shirt. Sometimes they'll wrap it around a pen, or fold it into the smallest possible square, or ball it up, or wrap it tightly around coins, or hide it in a crack in the bar mat. Please don't do any of this! We truly appreciate the tip as is, no need to spruce it up any. Doing so often creates more of a hassle for us.

If you ask for a really special drink, tip a bit more. This could apply to anything that's complicated/exotic, something they wouldn't normally make, something they looked up the recipe to make for you, had to get special ingredients for, etc. If they go above and beyond, show a little extra love.

Leaving only coins can be very insulting. If you get a drink and just leave a dime, nickel, or anything like that, you might just be better off leaving nothing. I personally will take any tip because I'm from the school of "it all adds up." Don't get me wrong—a dime tip is horrible, and I'll think you're a crappy tipper, but I most likely won't presume you meant to tell me to go f*#k myself. Other bartenders are different. Leaving a tip that small can sometimes be something a customer is doing intentionally to send a message to a bartender/server that they don't like them for whatever reason, so you doing it might just be unintentionally sending that message.

Don't say it, show it. The guy that announces "I'm a BIG tipper" or that tries to assure you he's going to "hook you up" never does. You're only making yourself look worse when you do that because now we're paying close attention when it comes time to see if you follow through or not. And we will remember it when you don't. Don't say it if you're not going to do it.

Don't fake it. If you say, "I'm going to come back later tonight and tip," we may give you the benefit of the doubt the first time you say it, but once you don't follow through we will not forget it. If you frequent a bar and do this and think you're getting away with it, you're an idiot. If you think that acting like you're shuffling through your wallet/pockets/purse searching for a tip while waiting for the bartender to turn their back so you can walk away–trust me–they know exactly what you're doing, and they despise you. It's the same as the crafty cheapskate that writes "CASH" on the gratuity line of their credit card receipt when they left no money at all. Again, we're not stupid. We know who you are and we hate you.

Don't ask the bartender how much you should leave for a tip if you're not prepared to leave that amount. I'll never get this. If you ask, "what do you want for a tip?" you'd better be ready to provide whatever they ask for, or you're going to look dumb. Do yourself (and the bartender) a favor and don't set yourself up for this awkward situation; just shut up and leave at least 20% of the total bill.

There's no need to announce what you left for a tip, or to try and show the bartender how much you left, or to ask for them to "remember you." Trust me. The bartender knows when you've left a good/bad tip and they will remember you for it. It always seems that the person that wants to show you how great their tip was more often than not left you a horrible tip. "Dude, you were so awesome! I just hooked you up with $5 on this $200 tab and want to make sure it goes directly to you cause you took such great care of us all night!" If this is you, please follow the same advice I gave in the previous tip and SHUT UP!

Always tip on the total amount of the ORIGINAL bill or the total sum of what your bill would have been before any freebies. Let's say you have a coupon that gets you a free entree. If your tab was $60 and the coupon takes it down to $40, your tip should still be based on the original amount ($60). Let's say you have a gift card for $100 and it takes your bill from $150 down to $50; you should still tip on the original amount ($150). Let's say your tab was $120, and the bartender decided to give you all a free round, which equated to $25 worth of drinks. You should at least tip on what the total would have been had you of had to pay for those drinks ($145).

Don't take *your* issues out on the bartender by cutting out their tip. If you bought drinks for some girls you were trying to impress/hook up with, and it didn't work out, that doesn't mean that now the bartender doesn't get a tip. If security throws you out for acting like an ass and they make you pay your tab first, that doesn't mean that you can now stiff the bartenders since you're getting tossed. If you and your boyfriend just got into a fight and the night is ruined, that doesn't mean that now you don't have to tip the bartender.

The bartender doesn't care about your excuse for not tipping. I've heard every excuse you can imagine, and none of them are acceptable. Some popular ones are, "I'm in college," "I'm on a tight budget," "I have kids," "I have bills due," "the economy is bad," "I don't have a job right now," "you make more money than I do," the list goes on and on. If you can't afford to tip, then you have no right being in a bar. There's a place where you can get all the booze you want without having to tip— it's called the liquor store.

If you're somewhere with an open bar, it's still customary to tip. These are common at work functions, weddings, bar mitzvahs, private parties, etc. Usually, at these kinds of events, the bartender will have a tip jar sitting out. Don't be cheap. I mean come on, you're already getting the booze for free!

> **PRO TIP:** *If you want to leave a big tip in a tip jar at one of these events make sure the bartender sees you do it. They'll take good care of you for the rest of the evening and won't think you're cheap when they don't see you tip later on that night.*

TAKING TIPPING TO THE NEXT LEVEL

Okay—so you've read all of these tips and want to know what it takes to go beyond just tipping "well" so can take your bar experience to the next level. Now we're talking. Here's the best way to do it:

Start out with your best tip first. It makes a great first impression that'll instantly make us remember you for future rounds. You don't have to keep every tip after that at the same level, just keep it good and you'll be great! Example: If your first round is $5, throw down $10 and say keep the change. The bartender will be super stoked and will take a good look at you so that they remember you; they may even alert the other bartenders that there's a "priority" in the house so that they'll take special care of you too. You can lower that tip to $2-$3 on each $5 round after that, and you'll still be a king/queen!

If you're using a credit card to pay at the end of the night, you can *still* make a great first impression. If you're starting a tab, unless we know you from previous visits we have no idea how great of a tipper you are. Sure, you could be awesome and leave an excellent 30% tip at the end, but that tip did nothing to fire up your service you were getting up to that point.

A good way to kick things off right if you are starting a tab is to hand the bartender a nice cash tip with your credit card to open your tab up. I've seen many people do this with stellar results. For example: Let's say you walk into a bar with three friends and you want to start a tab on your credit card, but also want to make sure you're getting treated like a priority. Have your credit card ready along with a $20 bill, hand them both to the bartender and say, "I'd like to start a tab on this credit card for the evening. We're going to be ordering quite a few rounds as well as some different snacks, and I just want to make sure you're well taken care of." You are now a top priority and will be getting absolute top tier service.

Leaving an additional tip to cover "hassles" will not only make up for any trouble, it'll make you a king/queen. If you drop a glass and break it, or your buddy knocks over his drink, and the bartender has to clean it up, throw down a couple of extra bucks while apologizing. If you made a mistake and ordered the wrong thing, or if the bartender sees you're not enjoying something and offers to replace it for you, leave a couple of extra bucks while thanking them. If you're ordering a lot of water, throw down a couple of bucks. ALL of these are behaviors that will get you major props from a bartender. It shows that you're self-aware, you have empathy, and that you care. If a bartender thinks you care about making sure they are taken care of, then they will care about making sure that you're treated well too.

Tipping to become a valued regular. So…you want to become a beloved regular at a specific bar? Try this! Go in for one drink and leave a $5 tip regardless of the price of the drink. There's no need to be too extreme and double that amount if you have two drinks the next time, but if you leave a minimum of either $5 or 20%, whichever is larger, we will remember you. If you combine this process with repeat visits, you're well on your way to becoming a regular we remember.

It's important to note though that just being a big tipper isn't what it takes to become a truly valued regular. There are plenty of regulars I serve that always throw around a ton of money and tip very well, but due to them lacking in other areas, they aren't customers that I feel compelled to bend over backward and go the extra mile for. This is usually because I have no real connection with them, as they've always used their money in a way that's created a barrier where they see me as just hired help catering to their needs without any real care, concern, or recognition for me as a person.

In contrast to that, if you combine the practice of tipping well with a bit of empathy, *now* you're the kind of customer bartenders love! If you convey that you understand when I'm busy by having patience and being respectful—and you tip well—then I love you! If you see that I'm dealing with a difficult customer or getting hassled and you show me that you "get" what's going on and you have my back, even if it's just a simple nod or a wink—and you tip well—I love you! If you're the kind of customer that always seems in control, knows what they're drinking, never gets too wasted or causes issues—and you tip well—I love you! And not only do I love you, I'll do just about anything to make sure you're having a killer night out with your friends.

There are regulars I serve daily that possess those qualities I just listed, and even though they might not tip as extravagantly as others, I'd do just about anything I can to take care of them. I've personally had someone watch the bar so I could drive to a store to get Tylenol for a guest. I've walked to another restaurant close by to get spicy mustard since we only had regular mustard and I knew a customer preferred the other kind. I once went and bought an entire pineapple at a market close by just so a guest could have it as a topping on a pizza. I've played the ultimate wingman and hooked up more guys and gals than I can count. Those are just a few of the many examples I could give you of the kind of service I'll provide for someone I really care about as a valued customer.

Keep that in mind when you're throwing money around. It doesn't take too much extra effort to show some human compassion; ask for their name and use it when talking to them, say please and thank you, and act like a human being. Those kinds of small things, combined with tipping well, take you from being cool to being awesome. If you want to be truly loved and revered as a valued customer, this is what it's all about.

Trust me when I tell you this: If a bartender loves you, you are *always* going to have a great experience at that bar.

The bottom line is that you don't have to break the bank to be a top priority in the bar. With a little respect, a little cash, and a little patience, you'll be well on your way to being treated as the awesome customer you're striving to be!

CHAPTER 5:

JESUS CHRIST, START A TAB!

I said it earlier in the book, and I'll say it again: The worst customers are the ones that order a drink, pay out on a credit card, order another drink, again pay out on a credit card, order another drink… you get it. You're causing the bartender to take way longer to handle what should be a quick, simple transaction, so here is the one golden rule you should always follow: **IF YOU DON'T WANT TO OPEN A TAB, BRING CASH!**

"How does it take longer," you ask? Let's take a look…

Let's say you want two more beers. You could say, "I'd like two more beers added to 'Jenkins.'" Two beers are grabbed from a cooler, popped open, and sat in front of you. BOOM. That took—what?—ten seconds at most? The bartender updates your tab accordingly, and you're done. It's a huge time-saver that results in everyone getting served faster!

Now let's look at it if you were swiping out with each payment. After you've asked for your two beers, I then have to take your credit card, wait to get access to a computer, ring it up, wait for it to print, then bring it back for you to sign it. Every. Single. Round. That takes perhaps a minute to do, maybe more/less depending on how busy the computer terminals are and how fast the printer works. The difference between a transaction taking ten seconds and one minute may not seem like much, but when you're taking care of hundreds of customers, and they all are also swiping out with each round, it quickly adds up. If ten people are doing this, instead of being able to serve them all in 1 minute and 40 seconds, it would instead take 10 minutes. That's a huge difference. Also, as a person that cares about the earth and its resources, I'd prefer not to waste all that paper.

So yes, tabs are so important that I've dedicated an entire chapter to understanding every aspect of how they work. If you plan on staying for a while, you should always start one (unless of course, you're paying cash). If your reason for not starting a tab is, "I don't trust myself not to put too much on it," or, "I can't because I always get too wasted and leave my credit card behind," well then, congratulations, you're *"that* guy/girl," and you seriously need to get your drinking and maturity in check.

So now that we've laid the foundation, here's everything else you need to know about how tabs work:

Know when it's time to pay up. Generally, you always pay out at the end of the night once you're ready to leave. There are some bars where you can run tabs for longer—say, weekly—but you usually have to be a regular to gain that level of trust at an establishment. There are also other factors like if you're staying at a hotel where you can just have your tab added to the bill you'll pay when you go to check out. It's your job to find out how it works at whatever place you're drinking.

Don't start tabs with "Gift Cards." Now, I'm not talking about gift cards sold specifically for the bar or restaurant; I'm talking about the branded prepaid cards (Visa, Mastercard, American Express, Discover) that can be used anywhere. My advice is just to avoid using these things at bars and restaurants altogether, here's why:

For starters, many bars won't accept them for running tabs. Why? Because there's no 'identity' attached to gift cards like there is with a credit/debit card or ID, so there's no value in holding one of these as leverage against an outstanding tab. They've more than likely already learned the hard way by being burned before by a person that's come in with a gift card that has a small balance on it (a balance that we can't see when we start a tab with one). They started a tab, racked up a couple of hundred bucks, then just walked out without paying, leaving behind a measly $10 gift card.

There's a second issue that you might not be aware of (most people aren't). Your gift card can get declined even if there is a balance on it. Why does this happen? It's because the credit card systems in most bars and restaurants are programmed to authorize 20% above the total check amount to account for a potential tip a customer may be leaving on the card. So, you're stoked because you have this $50 Visa Gift Card and your tab is $45, and you think you're covered. But when the computer checks to see if there's $54 on the card ($45, plus the potential 20% tip of $9), and finds that there isn't, it's going to get declined. It's better to skip the hassle and just use cash or a regular credit card like everyone else does.

Make sure your card is activated. It may sound stupid, but I've seen people overlook this. If it's a brand-new card, make sure you've called the toll free number and activated it before using it. It'll save you the embarrassment of having your card declined and the hassle of having to call and activate it in a noisy bar.

Find out if there is a minimum spend amount required to run your card. Some bars have a minimum you have to have on your tab before they'll run your credit card. This is for two reasons.

The first is because of what I described at the beginning of this chapter. Having a minimum keeps people from opening and closing out their one-drink tab over and over again. This, in turn, allows the bartenders to work efficiently, which translates into more customers getting served and the bar making more money.

The second reason is that bars and restaurants pay a fee every time a credit card gets swiped. It doesn't take a genius to realize that they'd want to keep those costs to a minimum, and they can do that by trying to keep the number of credit card swipes as low as they possibly can. As these growing fees continue to eat away at an establishment's bottom line, the answer is more often than not to begin raising prices to make up the loss. Without even realizing it, those "close out my card every single round" customers are in time making the drinks more expensive not only for themselves but for every single customer coming in. Wouldn't you rather just run a tab instead?

Hey! You didn't give me my card back! Yep, that's because most bars hold your credit card or ID while you have a tab. Don't worry; they're safely stored, usually in an alphabetical filing system, and you'll get it back once you close out at the end of the night.

***Know* who has your tab!** Don't be the amateur that starts freaking out on some random bartender about how they have your tab when that, in fact, isn't the case. This is not just a common nightly occurrence at busy bars; it's also one of the easiest mistakes rookies make that unbeknownst to them, sets them up to be completely humiliated in front of everyone.

First, pay attention to exactly which bartender or server started your tab for you. This is in case they are any issues later. Next, pay attention to where you started your tab. If the bar you're at has multiple levels and/or multiple bars, chances are that your tab can only be accessed at the exact bar where you started it. The same is true if you have a cocktail waitress or server. They are likely to have your tab, not the bar—meaning that only they have access to it to make changes or close it. Just adhering to those few simple tips will ensure that you're never left looking like the village idiot in front of your peers.

Find out how tabs are divided/shared if there are multiple bartenders working. At both places where I currently work, we all pool tips and work collectively. That means that we are all linked to the same shared info and that we all add to different tabs together as the night progresses. It's great for the customer because you don't have to order from the same bartender each time, and you don't have to close out your tab with the bartender who started it.

But not every bar will run on that same system. Some will require that you order from the bartender with whom you start your tab. You can find out what you're dealing with simply by asking, "Are you our bartender or can I order from anyone?"

Pay attention to how tabs are organized at the bar and order accordingly. Again, every place is different. Some organize by last name, some by which location you're in, some by laying out all the credit cards on a counter and using a visual reference to find your exact card, and so on. You can either directly ask what your tab name is under/how it's organized or, even better, just pay attention to what they ask you when you order your second round and adjust your future interactions accordingly. This is how seasoned bar customers do it.

Example: If you order a beer and I ask, "What's your last name?" then—BOOM—you now know the bar organizes by last names. In future rounds, you can say, "I'd like a Bud Light added to the 'Wilson' tab."

If you ask for a beer and I ask, "What does your credit card look like?" then—BOOM—you now know the bar organizes by what the card looks like. In future orders, you can now say, "I'd like a beer added to my tab. It's the gold AMEX card." It's that easy! When someone walks up to me and says, "Hi, can I please have two Bay Breezes? I have a tab open under "Williams," I know I'm dealing with a person that has their shit together, and I love that person. *Be* that person.

PRO TIP: *Bars can be loud, especially busy ones. If you have a difficult last name, try to make it easier on the bartender. If it's pronounced "He-she" but spelled "Xiechi," you gotta help us out a bit. If you just keep yelling that your last name is "He-she" over and over, I'm going to keep looking in the "H" section for your tab. Better to say, "I'd like to close the 'He-she' tab. 'X, I, E.'"*

Another good idea is to have your ID on hand and point to your last name. I LOVE when someone does this because it makes it so much easier to find the correct tab quickly. The same idea applies if you have a common last name, like "Smith." If that's the case, then it's worth stating, "My last name is Smith, first name Mike." Or if you're there with your brother/sister and you have separate tabs, let the bartender know that when you start your tab. They'll love you for making their life easier.

ALWAYS give a direct answer to the *exact* question the bartender is asking you. It seems like such a simple concept, but sadly it isn't. Here's just one example of a typical *excruciating* conversation that takes place multiple times every night:

> **Young Customer:** Can you add a Bud Light to my tab?
>
> **Me:** Sure, what's your last name?
>
> **Young Customer:** It's a green Capital One card!
>
> **Me:** Okay, but what's the last name?

Young Customer: My name is Mike!

Me: Okay, your last name is Mike?

Young Customer: No, that's my first name!

Me: What's your last name?

Young Customer: Johnson!

It's *ridiculous*. It might sound like I'm exaggerating, but I assure you I'm not. The point is that we ask you a specific question for a reason, so if we ask you one *just answer the damn question!*

Don't use someone else's credit card or put drinks on someone else's tab. This is a huge no-no. Unless that person has specifically told the bartender that it's okay for you to do so, don't even try. Start your own tab, or let the person who did start the tab field the ordering.

Transferring a tab you've started at the bar to a table. So you're at the bar for an hour while you're waiting for a table to be ready. You've had a few rounds and an appetizer, and now the hostess is telling you that your table is ready. Can you just transfer your tab to the table?! Often you can, but it's not the classy thing to do. The bartender who's been taking care of you for the last hour should at least get tipped for the work they did, so the best bet is to always close out with the bar first. If you've picked up any knowledge from this book so far, then you should be ready and prepared to handle the tab quickly and efficiently.

PRO TIP: *Don't ever just get up and take drinks you've ordered from the bar while waiting for a table to said table before either closing out or speaking with the bartender first. This happens quite often and it's a pain in the ass for the bartender, who has to leave their post to find you and bring you your tab. This can be especially daunting if it's a large restaurant or bar that has multiple levels or dining rooms. We're not psychic, so finding you means wandering around until we do.*

Clarify how you'd like to close your tab when it's time. Starting a tab on a credit card does not mean you have to use that card to pay at the end of the night. Many people start a tab on a card and then close it out with cash, or with a different card, or split amongst three of their friend's credit cards, etc. Be clear about what you want. If you say, "Can you please close the "Jones tab?" that signifies that you want the whole bill run on your card. If you'd prefer to pay with cash, say so: "I have a tab under 'Jones' that I'd like to pay with cash."

PRO TIP: *If your check is presented to you in a booklet you can expedite the payment process by making sure your cash or credit card is visible. This lets your bartender/server know that you're ready to pay. Many payment booklets come with a credit card slot designated just for this specific purpose.*

Don't argue about what's on your tab. If you do, you better be *100% sure* it's stuff you really didn't order. I see people all the time that are shocked when they get their tab: "There's *no way* I drank that many beers!" Yup, you sure did, buddy. You also bought shots for every friend you ran into, and every girl you encountered all night long.

Don't ask for cash back. In case you weren't aware, you're at a *bar*, not an ATM. or grocery store. If you need cash, *go to an ATM. or grocery store.*

Don't forget to sign your receipt, add gratuity, and *return the pen*. Even if you're going to leave a cash tip (which is great), it's always a good idea to make sure you sign your receipt and write clearly. If your plan is to stiff the bartender, well, there's a special place in hell for you (it's the same pit you go to when you steal bartenders pens!).

Make sure you're taking the right copy! This is very important, and *a lot* of people screw this up when they're trashed. If you're given a slip to sign and there are two copies, make sure you take the right one. Usually, the one you're supposed to leave behind will say something like "merchant copy" at the bottom, and the one you're supposed to take will say something like "customer copy." Taking the wrong one can mean that the bartenders working won't be able to get the tip you intended on leaving them, which means you just accidentally stiffed them.

Remember where you placed your credit/debit card/ID after you close your tab. If accusing the wrong bartender/server of having your tab is the first best way to make a fool of yourself, then this is without a doubt a very close second. If I told you the number of newbs that accuse us of not returning their credit card, only to later find it in their pocket, their friend's wallet, their cleavage, the floor, or best of all THEIR HAND, you'd never believe me. Seriously, don't even begin to start accusing someone of theft until you've checked all of those locations first.

If you forget to close your tab don't panic. This is a *very* common occurrence. Even if the bar's already closed, they have a tried and true method of holding credit cards/ID's in a safe place until the person that left it comes to pick it up the next day. Just be aware that in most cases you *will not* be able to leave a tip on your credit card the next day due to the payment info already being processed and closed out at the end of the previous night.

A nice thing to do is bring some cash and leave it for the bartenders that worked that night, or just remember to try and make it up to them the next time you come.

> **PRO TIP:** *Some bars have a policy of placing a specific amount of gratuity on your tab if you forget to close it out and leave your card there. Usually, there will be a sign posted somewhere on the wall that says something like, "A 20% gratuity will be added to any tabs left overnight." Maybe they don't have a sign at all and just do it. If you want to know a bar's policy, just ask.*

Don't call the next morning freaking out over "pending" charges shown on your account. This will just show that you're inexperienced at life and that you have no idea how credit/debit cards work. Sometimes when you go to open a tab, a bar or restaurant will pre-authorize your card. This is done to make sure that it's a valid, working card, and that your account has enough money in it to cover your bill as well as any gratuity that might be added. Depending on certain factors, these pre-authorizations at times can be higher than what your actual bill ends up being. It could also be a case where you had a tab going on a card, but you chose to use cash to pay for everything. IT'S OKAY! These pre-authorizations ARE NOT charges, and they usually go away in one to three days. Once that occurs, the *actual* amount of your bill will then appear (unless you paid cash, in which case it'll just go away completely).

If the bartender *does* misplace your tab/credit card. Hey, we're all humans, and we can all make mistakes. It's rare to lose a credit card behind the bar, but I have seen it happen. More specifically, I'd say I've seen it about four times in all the years I've been bartending. In each of those times, the card turned up later. One time, it had slid under the printer; one time it fell on the floor and got wedged in the cabinet molding (the odds of it landing that way had to of been over 1:1,000,000). The other two were similarly random occurrences.

The point I'm making is that this sort of thing doesn't happen often. And if it DOES, stay calm. Chances are it will turn up once the bar closes. Leave your phone number with the bartender/manager and if you don't hear back from them, call back about thirty minutes after closing and see if there's an update. If you're cool and calm, most reputable bars will take very good care of you for the inconvenience.

This may seem like a daunting amount of information for something as basic as starting a tab, but I assure you it's pretty simple. Once you've done it a few times you'll be a pro at it!

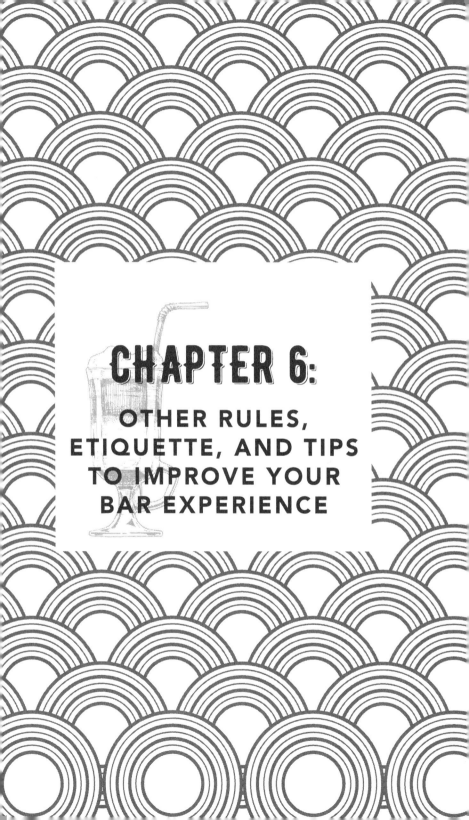

CHAPTER 6:
OTHER RULES, ETIQUETTE, AND TIPS TO IMPROVE YOUR BAR EXPERIENCE

Okay, so at this point in the book, we've covered pretty much all the basics. In this section, I'm going to go over "all of the rest" of what you'll need to know for just about every kind of scenario/situation you'll be faced with while out drinking, and how to handle it the right way.

Sitting at the bar or at tables in the bar. Yes, there is a right way and a wrong way to sit at a bar or at tables in a bar. I'm going to cover the basics for you in these next few sections.

The first step, assuming the bar isn't packed, is picking a clean spot to sit. If you go into a bar and there are twenty seats open, two of which still have dishes and glasses sitting there, do not pick those two seats. For some reason this is a "thing," and I can't for the life of me figure out why. People that make this mistake unknowingly have already sent a clear message to the bartender about what kind of customer they're going to be. (Hint: not a good one!) So getting off to a great start is as easy as picking a clean spot.

If the bar is packed, and two seats just opened up, it is okay to head over and immediately snag those spots even if they're dirty. The best way to do this is to stand behind the seats (this shows other patrons you've claimed the now open spots) and wait a second for the bartender to see you. Just you doing that will register to them that you're waiting for those two seats and they'll clean them up for you a.s.a.p.

Picking a seat the right way. Most people go to bars/restaurants in pairs. With that thought in mind, there's a very courteous way to select seats at a bar. The general rule is to never leave a single seat open if you can avoid it. This allows better spacing so that other patrons can have access to the bar and/or bar seating as well.

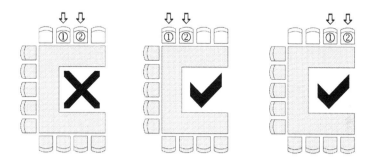

If you're in a group of three, try to snag an area of the bar where the seat placement will create a natural triangle shape. This is optimal for both space and conversation so you don't have two people on the outside shouting across a person in the middle who's left constantly having to turn their body left and right. Corners are perfect for this!

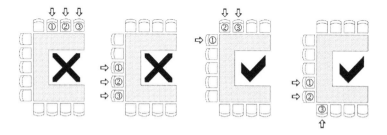

If a corner isn't available, it's best to have two people sit while the third stands in the middle just behind them.

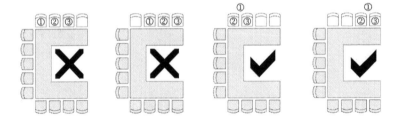

For groups larger than three, I suggest getting a table, as conversation can become difficult to follow the more spread out your group is. This is especially true if the bar you're in is a loud one.

Be aware of others and be courteous and accommodating whenever possible. Let's say you and your friend are out and that you've snagged the last two seats at a packed bar and ordered some food. Over the course of you being there, one seat has opened up on each side of you. You now see a couple walking around scanning the bar looking for a place to sit. What's the right thing to do?! The answer is to motion them over and offer to slide down a seat so they can sit down. I see kind people do this quite often and it many times leads to a round of drinks getting bought for them, or new friendships getting formed. That doesn't mean you should ever do it expecting anything in return; you should do it because it's the right thing to do.

To add to that, the same rule applies at a bar as it does in you're on a bus or subway. Guys, this especially pertains to you. If you see an elderly person, a pregnant woman, or a handicapped person trying to find a place to sit, it's a very kind and courteous gesture to offer them your seat until they can get one of their own. I mean, come on, didn't your momma raise you with some manners?!

Tables in a bar: Do you have a server or not?!
Every bar operates differently. Some bars have tables; some don't. For the bars that do, sometimes the tables are just there for open seating, and sometimes there's a server working those tables. If you don't have a server and the tables are just open, then it's totally fine for you to keep ordering your drinks up at the bar. If you do have a server, then you should be ordering from them.

Bar servers make their entire living off of the income they generate from those tables—the same as a regular server does in a typical restaurant. The general rule is that if you don't want a server to serve you then don't sit at their table.

Moving around tables/chairs to suit your needs.
Don't just go in and start rearranging everything like you own the place. Always ask first. Without even realizing it, you could totally be screwing over a server, bartender, or another customer by moving the furniture around. If you need an extra chair or table to accommodate your growing group, ask for one.

This rule also applies to changing the atmosphere without asking. It always amazes me how self-centered a person can be when they're in a room full of a hundred people and have no problem walking over and turning the thermostat up or down, opening/closing blinds, changing a TV, turning fans off/on, turning lights up/down/off, etc. Don't ever assume it's alright to change the entire environment just to suit your needs—at the very least, ask permission first.

Placing your belongings on another table. It's rude. You're taking up space that doesn't belong to you. This includes placing your dirty dishes or glasses on a table that isn't yours once you're finished with them. A server, bartender, or busser will gladly remove them for you once you're ready.

Keep your coat on the back of your chair and any belongings you have either under your chair, under your table, or on your lap. If you're in a booth as opposed to a table, be mindful of hanging your coats/jackets over the top in a way that people can't sit at the table behind you. Did you bring so much stuff with you that you don't have enough space in any of those locations I suggested?! If the answer is yes, then you're doing life all wrong!

Leaving coasters or napkins sitting on drinks. You may have seen this before and wondered what the heck this is all about. Leaving a napkin or coaster over the top of a glass signals that the person is coming right back. People flying solo for the evening find this trick especially useful. If they have to get up and use the bathroom or run out for a smoke, this is how they can make sure their drink doesn't get thrown away or their seat taken. DON'T ABUSE THIS. I dealt with a customer one time that was super pissed when he came back to find that his seat and drink were both gone. The problem? He had left for over an hour and even admitted that he walked home to make food and planned on coming back after he ate. He didn't get at all why there was anything wrong with that. Don't be that guy.

If you're at a bar/club that has bathroom attendants. Their job is to stand in a bathroom all night and listen to you shit. Well, not really. Their *real* job is to provide nice extras for your evening like cologne/perfume, tampons, makeup remover, gum, mints, condoms, combs, towels, etc. If you take *anything* they have to offer, it's customary to at least leave a dollar or two as a tip.

Don't climb or stand on the bar. I don't care how impressive you think it is, or how cool of a Snapchat it's going to make. I don't care that you just wanted to get your buddies attention on the other side of the bar. All I know is that you're getting tossed outside *immediately*.

Don't bring in outside food or drink. EVER. This is tacky and completely unacceptable. Some counties even have laws against outside food or drink, which are there for your own safety. We don't know if that coffee cup you're bringing in has regular coffee in it or a spiked coffee. Even worse is the person that thinks it's okay to bring in a flask of booze and add it to the Coke they ordered. Not only do you look extremely cheap to all your friends, but at some point you'll get caught— and when that time comes, you could very well get banned from that bar for life.

As for food, if I have to tell you why it's not okay to bring a Subway footlong sub into a restaurant/bar and open it up and eat it at the bar or a table, then you should probably just not ever go out at all. Ever. Like for real, do the world a favor and just stay home *forever*.

Don't discuss religion or politics. Seriously, save those topics for more private areas. Even older bar regulars seem to miss the boat on this one at times. If you're going for a night out to have fun, keep that in mind. The problem with discussing those two topics, or any hot-button issue (abortion, racism, terrorism, etc.), is that they'll more often than not lead to arguments when paired with alcohol. Then from there to physical fights. As human beings spinning around the sun on a vast and varied earth, we all have our individual opinions and feelings—some extreme, some not. Challenging the views of someone else, or aggressively throwing yours out there, is not a way to have a positive experience on a Friday night out with friends, old or new.

Smoking/Vaping/Chewing Tobacco/etc. Always find out the rules before you begin partaking in any of these things. Even if you're on a patio and think it's okay, it may not be. For example, my city has very specific rules about what constitutes an outdoor space, and some of them are pretty counterintuitive. So to be safe, always ask.

Vaping is the latest trend, and unfortunately, due to many vapers abusing the privilege it's rapidly becoming banned in public places across the country.

Chewing tobacco is generally accepted everywhere. If you're going to do it at least ask for a plastic cup and place some cocktail napkins in it to absorb all the spit. When it's time to leave take it with you and dispose of it in a proper receptacle. It is absolutely *not* okay to leave it sitting on your table.

Cellphone/smartphone use. As each year passes by, I notice more and more that people, especially young ones, are engrossed in their phones while they're out with friends. They spend no time talking to each other, getting to know each other, or making new friends—you know, the reasons people go to a bar.

Try to limit your smartphone use to a minimum, and I promise you you'll have a much more enjoyable night. Years from now when you're looking back, your friendships—which can only develop through real in-depth communication—will be all that matters. I assure you that you won't miss having a picture of every single shot you've done in college. And for the love of God, if you're placing an order at the bar, please put your phone away for twenty seconds and show the bartender some respect.

Phone charging. So you're out drinking, and your phone's about to die. If you need some extra battery life for something important—say, calling an Uber later or meeting back up with friends—you're in luck as many bars do offer charging areas. These can range from a bunch of outlets that customers have access to, to an area behind the bar where bartenders control the charging of a customer's phone. The general rule there is to be respectful. Once the bartender has been kind enough to plug your phone in and charge it for you, don't keep asking them to check and see if your buddy texted you back yet. Don't keep asking for an update on your battery percentage. They were kind enough to hook you up with some juice—don't abuse it.

TVs in bars. Many bars offer TVs for patrons to watch while they're out drinking and enjoying their evening. There are a few unspoken guidelines to how these work, and it's dependent really on a few different factors. I'll just try to give you the basics.

First is a general rule most bars have of not allowing "news" to be on TVs in the bar. This is because it's too depressing. The second rule is to keep it appropriate. The U.F.C. fight is fine to have on in a bar that's comprised of all adults (there are *plenty* of bars that pay for these P.P.V. events and advertise specifically for them). However, if you're in a bar that doubles as a restaurant, or where there are older people or families around, it's not appropriate. Nobody wants to sit and eat their food while watching someone bleeding profusely all over a mat. This all leads back to why it's important to plan out which bar you want to go to based on what you want to do for the evening.

With bar TVs, usually it's a "first come, first served" situation. Whoever was there first and asked for a TV to be turned to a specific event gets to watch said event. It's also a general rule before just switching a TV to something new to ask around and see if anyone was watching what was on there first. If someone was, find another TV you can watch (if there's more than one) or move on to another bar.

> **PRO TIP:** *If you're coming into a bar to watch a specific sporting event, scan around the room and check out what's on the TV's before finding a seat. Then, pick a seat where you have a great view of that TV. This is a far better approach than just quickly sitting down in a random spot and then requesting TVs be switched around to accommodate your location.*

Don't expect *anything* for free. It doesn't matter if you've spent a ton of money and your tab is over $300, you're not entitled to *anything* more than any other customer. I don't care how much you've spent—if you're acting like an entitled ass all night and demanding free things you'll get *nothing*. If I *do* happen to have an extra drink that I can give away, I assure you it's going to go to the cool chill guy that's been respectful all night, even if his tab is only at $10. That goes for sodas, too. Yes, some bars will give a D.D. (designated driver) a free soda, but not all of them. Don't expect it.

If you have a special arrangement with another bartender keep it to yourself. That could mean a special price they give you, a bigger sized or stronger drink, or using a call liquor while charging you for rail. If you want that deal, then make sure you order from them. It's incredibly rude to ask another bartender to match it, and in many cases, you could be getting your "hook up" in big trouble.

I can't tell you how many times I've heard, "The other bartender makes my drink stronger," "When I come on Wednesday nights the bartender always gives me top shelf for the price of rail," or "Karen always gives me a free shot with each beer I order." By doing anything like this, you've just put all of us in a very uncomfortable position. Unbeknownst to general guests, it's very common for a bartender to double as a bar manager. This is true at both places I currently bartend at, and there's nothing that separates them visually from a regular bartender, so you'd have no idea you were spilling the beans to a manager unless they told you.

Free samples. Here is a GREAT way to try something to see if you like it before committing to ordering an entire drink. Bars that have a lot of different beers on tap are usually pretty open to letting you try a little taste of one or two of them before you decide. The same holds true of places that offer a variety of different wine. It's perfectly acceptable to ask for a small taste (if it's something that's available by the glass and not only by the bottle). The important thing here is NOT to abuse this. Trying ten different beers before ordering one is a dick move.

> **PRO TIP:** *See if they offer a sample rack or flight. This is a wonderful way to get to try all of the different offerings a place has and to truly figure out what you like. It's especially great if you're inexperienced, and still awesome even if you're not. Even after almost two decades of experienced drinking, I've found some of my favorite whiskeys by trying flights.*

Free food. Many bars offer free food as an incentive to bring in guests on certain days of the week to build business. This can range from a few snacks placed around the bar, to entire free buffets where you serve yourself. These kinds of events often attract the worst kinds of customers. Everyone hates the guy that comes in, eats eight plates of food, buys nothing, tips nothing, then leaves. This person may just be the *ultimate* asshole.

If you're at one of these, help yourself and enjoy. Just follow these few guidelines. The first is that you have to order something. Often these promotions will run along with cheap drink specials, so you have no excuse not to. The second is to be courteous to other guests and share. It's not cool at all to dump the entire pan of chicken wings on your plate leaving none for anyone else. The third is never to pack up the food and take it with you. It's only meant to be eaten there by guests that are patrons of the bar. The fourth and last one, *tip*.

If you have a coupon, know how the discount applies. A popular example of this is coupons where you get, say, $10 off if you spend $50. You order $30 in food and $20 in drinks and think you're good to go, only to find out when you try to use the coupon that it clearly says on the back that alcohol doesn't apply, and you have to order $50 in *food* to get the discount. Always read the fine print, and if that doesn't clarify it for you then ask your bartender/server before you order.

Returning drinks. There's a fine line of acceptability here. If your order came out wrong, then yes, it's okay if you return it. If it's in a dirty or broken glass, then *absolutely* return it. However, if it just isn't something you like that much then, in most cases, it can be pretty classless to send it back. Going out on a limb and trying something new is a part of life, and that's a risk that *you* are deciding to take, so why should a business have to pay if you made a bad decision? Sometimes you'll like things; sometimes you won't—that's life. If you try something new and don't like it, the right thing to do is just to finish the drink and make a mental note never to order that again.

Don't complain if you don't want it fixed. If you're going to complain about something, be it food or drink, don't deny the bar's offer to fix it. If you hate something or if it was made wrong then, sure, speak up and let us either fix it for you ourselves or have a manager come over and make it right.

Don't overstay after you've paid. Once you've paid your tab, it's okay to stay for a bit—but don't abuse it. Buying a few things does not buy your rent for the rest of the evening, even if you tipped well. Probably the worst example I've ever seen of this was when I was a server at a well-known BBQ restaurant. A nice older lady would come in by herself at lunchtime carrying this huge shopping bag. She'd sit at a table in my section, order a simple sandwich and Coke, quickly eat it and pay out, leaving me a $6 tip on a $12 check. A 50% tip?! That's awesome! But then she'd proceed to stay well into the dinner shift (almost four more hours), working on whatever project she brought with her! While her tip she left was good in theory, her being there actually caused a loss of money because that table could have been flipped at least four more times had she left after she was finished eating.

That's an extreme example, but people do commonly do this to a lesser extent. It's *especially* inconsiderate when you're drinking/dining at a time where there's a waiting list for people to get tables or bar space. After you've paid, it's time to get your belongings together and move on.

Don't take a seat too early. Let's say you and your friend arrive and you're waiting for five other people to join you. You know they're not going to be here for another hour or more, but you and your friend decide to grab a table for seven anyway so that you can sit and catch up in the meantime. This is bad, especially if this is during a time when a restaurant or bar is at their peak business (like a Friday or Saturday night). You're taking up space in the servers section and more importantly, from other potential customers that are also waiting to sit down. Holding a seat for a couple of minutes, sure. Ten minutes or more, no way. It's first come, first served.

Ordering nothing. I've never understood why people do this. Sometimes somebody will just sit at the bar and say they're hanging out for a while because they have "nothing better to do." They'll have a couple of waters, take up a spot at the bar for an hour or two, and then just leave with no tip. Even worse, I've seen entire parties of eight or more that have come and sat at the bar while waiting for a table to be ready. They won't order anything at all and are just using the spots at the bar as places to sit and rest while they wait. Those seats they're taking up are how bartenders make their income, so not only are they preventing them from doing that, they're also blocking space from customers that would like to use them to order food or drinks. Don't ever do this.

Drink specials may only be available in certain locations of the bar/restaurant. Many establishments offer a happy hour through the week. They do it to drive business to certain areas, like the bar, during non-peak business hours. With that said, it is incredibly tacky to, let's say, go from the table you're eating at in the restaurant over to the bar to order your drinks, only to bring them back to the table with you because they have a happy hour there and your beer is a dollar cheaper. In fact, many places have very strict rules about this. It's quite simple: If you want the drink special, that's available in a certain area of the bar, then sit there.

Don't lie about your intentions. Don't know what that has to do with anything?! Let me give you an example: A place I bartend at has a small outdoor patio set up for dining with very limited seating. It's extremely popular, especially when the weather's great. People will wait upwards of two hours just to have a seat out there when there are plenty of open seats indoors. To meet the demand, we have a very simple rule in place: You can only sit out there if you're ordering food. If we didn't have the rule, then people would just sit out there and take up a table for three hours only sipping a beer or two and basking in the warm weather.

So what do people do? The shitty ones just lie. When told specifically at the host stand that they must order food if they sit on the patio they just say, "Oh, we will." Then once the server arrives and asks to take their order, they think it's hilarious to just say, "Ohh, we said we were going to order food so we could sit out here. We just want to have a couple of sodas and catch up in the nice weather." If you do this, you are a self-centered asshole. If a restaurant or bar has any rules for sitting in/entering an area, please follow them.

Don't ask the bartender how much money they make. Not only is it extremely rude, it's none of your business!

Live music. Many bars have nights of the week where they feature live music. This can range from a full band playing cover songs to a lone solo artist with an acoustic singing original material, to open mic nights or karaoke. Always be respectful to the people performing. I've seen it all—from people that have loudly started "booing" a young girl playing an acoustic, to people that have asked to have the TV's sound turned up louder than a person playing. In case you're unaware, let me be clear: It's never okay to make fun of or heckle someone performing. If you're not in the mood for music, get up and go somewhere else.

Profanity. Try to keep it at a minimum. Many bars also double as restaurants, and there are often families or smaller children within earshot. Even if there aren't, dropping the "f-bomb" left and right just looks immature.

Don't bring in any weapons. Yeah, I have to mention this because people try to do it. Don't try to bring a bat, a baton, handcuffs, a stun gun, mace, knives, guns, or bombs into a bar or restaurant.

Don't *ever* fight inside the bar. When fights break out, 99% of the time all the participants get thrown out. Security won't stand around listening to who said what, who swung first, or who started it. If you have had more than one issue with getting into fights at the same bar, you're probably well on your way to being banned. I'm not saying you should stand there and just take an ass kicking—if someone takes a swing at you then, by all means, defend yourself. What I'm *strongly* suggesting is that if you can in anyway avoid it then take that option instead.

Children/babies in bars. Sad this even has to be said, but a bar is not a place for children. Just because a bar legally allows a child in there at certain times does not mean you should bring them there. Regardless of what time of day it is, bars are areas where people have adult conversations, so there's always going to be a greater chance of a child hearing things they shouldn't hear.

Many young parents also overlook how sensitive a child's ears are to noise. Babies' ears, in particular, are extremely susceptible to this. The general rule that most researchers in the field have agreed upon is that if the bar noise is low enough that you and a pal can talk comfortably without having to raise your voice at all, then it's okay. Anything louder than that and you could begin causing irreversible damage to your baby's hearing.

Know the signs if you're striking out. This is one of the worst things to witness—*holy mother of God*. Guys, this is pretty much 99% directed at you. You don't EVER want to be the guy that is being too aggressive in hitting on girls at a bar. If she says no, or asks you to stop, or is ignoring you, trying harder always leads to an even worse failure. It's time to move on. Seriously. It's pretty much the most cringe-worthy thing we witness as bartenders, and we see it frequently. Know the signs and be self-aware. Stop embarrassing yourself.

Pretty much everything covered in this chapter comes down to having very basic respect. Once you begin to develop that, *every* area in your life will improve dramatically.

CHAPTER 7:

BALANCING DRINKING AND YOUR HEALTH

So it's safe to say at this point in the book you now know all there is to know about how to be a master of the bar experience, so, we're done here, right?! Sorry, you're not getting away that easy. I'll never be able to get a full night's sleep again if I don't throw in at least one section that addresses some serious potential risks drinking can have on your health. You're almost to the end, so just take a minute and hear me out. I haven't steered you wrong yet, have I?!

I'm not going to beat around the bush; the truth is that alcohol can have serious consequences on your body and overall health. I'm sure you've heard of extreme cases of death that have come from driving while intoxicated, the perils of alcohol addiction, the potential for alcohol poisoning, the risk of serious illnesses like heart disease, high blood pressure, stroke, liver disease, or cancer. It's no joke, and I'd be doing you a huge disservice if I just glossed over all of that.

As a new drinker just starting out, it's important to keep in mind how the C.D.C. (Centers for Disease Control) defines excessive drinking. For women, it is defined as having four or more drinks during a single occasion, or eight or more drinks per week; if you're a man, having five or more drinks during a single occasion, or fifteen or more drinks per week is excessive. It doesn't take much to hit that weekly mark if you're having a couple of drinks every few nights. Once you're at that level of alcohol intake, you begin to place yourself at a much higher risk of encountering one or more of those serious issues I outlined.

Like everything, though, there is a middle ground;

moderation is the key here. What is moderation you ask?! For an adult male it's two standard drinks per day, and for a female, it's one standard drink per day. As for what a "standard drink" is, I'm sorry to tell you that the 20 oz. glass of wine you're crushing nightly won't fly—not even close. A standard drink is either a 5 oz. glass of wine, a 12 oz. beer, or 1.5 oz. shot of liquor.

That brings us to one of the most commonly overlooked side effects of drinking: WEIGHT GAIN. Even if you're just a moderate drinker, those calories can really begin to add up. Sure, it might not hit you in your early 20's while your metabolism is high, but once you creep into your late 20's and early 30's, that weight gain will begin to take its toll.

So the question is, why does this happen? And more importantly, what can you do to prevent it as much as you possibly can without having to give up drinking?

Let's start by tackling that first question.

Weight Gain

Contrary to what many believe, weight gain from alcohol *does not* just come from the calories you're taking in from the drinks themselves. Yes, that's *absolutely* something you have to pay attention to, but there's far more than just the calories themselves that are wreaking havoc on your body. The biggest issue that's often overlooked is that when you're drinking your body will *always* make alcohol its processing priority—ahead of burning fat, protein, carbohydrates, or even sugar. This equates to what is essentially a "pause" that takes place with your metabolism, and the result of this "pause" is that whatever food you've recently eaten ends up getting stored in your body as fat as opposed to being burned off. In addition to that, when consuming alcohol, your body has a much harder time burning fat that's *already there*, along with a particularly damning decrease in fat being burned in your stomach area. This isn't really all that surprising when you consider how many drinkers have "beer bellies"—the term exists for a reason!

Then, of course, there is the issue of the calories you're consuming from the alcohol itself, and any mixers added to it. Alcohol is the second most calorie dense macronutrient, coming in at seven calories per gram (pure fat is the first at nine calories per gram), and it's important to note that these alcohol calories contain no beneficial nutrients, vitamins, or minerals. Mixers can sometimes provide more calories than the booze itself does! Many people would be shocked if they knew how many calories they're taking in during a drinking session.

So, what *is* the caloric content of some of the most popular drinks? Let's take a look!

Straight liquor:

1.5 oz. (a standard "shot") of straight vodka/rum/gin/whiskey = 100 calories

I thought it'd be good to show a few other popular liquor options as well. People usually say that higher proof equals higher calories, but you'll see that that's not always the case.

1.5 oz. Captain Morgan (100 proof) = 122 calories

1.5 oz. Goldschlager (87 proof) = 143 calories

1.5 oz. Jägermeister (70 proof) = 150 calories

1.5 oz. Rumple Minze (100 proof) = 164 calories

1.5 oz. Bacardi 151 (151 proof) = 183 calories

1.5 oz. Everclear (190 proof) = 226 calories

Various drinks
Keep in mind that these numbers depend on the size of your beverage and the exact recipes that a bar is using, which can vary wildly:

5 oz. glass of wine = 110-300 calories

Pint (16 oz.) light beer = 135 calories

Pint (16 oz.) regular beer = 195 calories

9 oz. White Russian = 300-450 calories

12 oz. Long Island Iced Tea = 300-550 calories

9 oz. Tropical Drink (i.e. Hurricane/Mai Tai/etc.) = 300-600 calories

12 oz. Mudslide = 400-600 calories

12 oz. Margarita = 300-700 calories (depends on size, pour count, frozen/rocks, brand of sour mix, and salt.)

To compare, let's look at the calorie content of some popular types of "junk" food:

1 oz. bag of Lays potato chips = 160 calories

1 Taco Bell crunchy taco = 170 calories

1 standard size Snickers bar = 215 calories

1 small side of McDonald's french fries = 230 calories

1 slice of plain yellow cake = 240 calories

1 Dunkin Donuts glazed donut = 260 calories

1 typical average sized slice of cheese pizza = 275 calories

1 medium sized blueberry muffin = 430 calories

1 Big Mac burger from McDonald's = 560 calories

After seeing those numbers, consider for a second that the standard suggested daily calorie intake is typically 2,000 calories for an adult female and about 2,500 calories for an adult male. Even just one drink accounts for a measurable percentage of your suggested daily calorie intake!

Here are a few shocking facts based on all that data:

- If you drink an average-sized (750ml) bottle of red wine before bed, while also eating two slices of cheese pizza, you've just tacked on at least 1,300 calories to your daily intake! That number could be even higher depending on what kind of wine you're drinking and how big the slices of pizza are!

- If you had six regular beers and followed that up with a large McDonald's Big Mac Value Meal, you just tacked on 2,550 calories to your day (almost the equivalent of twelve Snickers bars)!

- If you drink five White Russians in one night, you'll consume the same amount of calories as about eight Dunkin Donuts glazed donuts!

- If you drink five frozen margaritas in one night, you'll take in the same number of calories you'd of received from thirteen small sides of McDonald's french fries, or seventeen Taco Bell crunchy tacos, or nineteen small bags of Lays potato chips!

Holy shit, that's *insane!* Keep in mind those numbers are all *in addition* to the effects of your body ceasing to process all the food you'd consumed *prior* to taking in these new calories.

As if the calories themselves weren't enough, the **amount of sugar** that's found even just in the alcohol itself, without any mixers, can be *staggering*. A 1.5 oz. shot of Fireball has 11 grams of sugar in it. A 1.5 oz. shot of Jägermeister has an *unbelievable 16.4 grams of sugar* in it (that's a full tablespoon of sugar)! Keep in mind that according to the American Heart Association, the maximum amount of sugars you should eat in an **entire day** are 25 grams if you're a female, and 37.5 grams if you're a male.

Now you can clearly see why it's so easy to pack on the pounds as a result of drinking.

So what's the best way to get around this? What's the best way to avoid putting on weight while moderately enjoying some booze? Those are great questions! Here are some helpful tips that'll get you on the right track:

Always eat a good meal before you go out drinking. Don't make the mistake of not eating in order to make room for booze, as trading food calories for booze calories will almost always backfire. That's because the majority of cocktails are packed with simple carbohydrates, which will cause your blood sugar to soar, followed shortly after by a crash. When this crash occurs your body will be screaming to be fed, and let's be real, what kind of food are you going to reach for at that point in the evening? That's right; garbage.

To prevent this, experts suggest eating a meal packed with foods that provide long-lasting energy before you begin drinking. These include foods high in protein, healthy fat, and fiber. Protein shakes are an excellent option, as are apples with almond butter, cottage cheese, eggs, tuna, lentils, quinoa, and Greek yogurt with blueberries.

"Saving up" your drinks from the week to use all on one night is *bad*. For example, if you skip drinking from Sunday to Friday just so you can have seven drinks on Saturday, it will have a much bigger effect on your body than if you'd had one or two drinks per day throughout the week. The reason is that when you take in that many drinks in one night, your body is now faced with having to process hundreds of calories before it can continue its normal job of breaking down food calories or stored fat.

You've probably made it even worse by using Saturday night as your "cheat night" for food too, creating the perfect storm of weight gain. Experts say that even just having four drinks on one night of the week can easily result in a 10 lb. weight gain over the course of a year. That's without any added junk food, too. Yikes!

Dark beer has fewer calories than regular beer. You can save about 25 calories per beer by choosing a dark beer over a regular beer.

White wine has fewer calories than red wine. You can shave about ten calories per glass off by just choosing white wine or a rosé!

> **PRO TIP:** *Sticking to lighter colored or clear drinks like white wine, vodka, etc. will result in you consuming fewer congeners. Studies have shown that congeners (which are substances that are produced during fermentation) may, in fact, play a large part in how bad your hangover is the next morning.*

Sweeter drinks will make you hungrier. Your blood sugar skyrockets much higher when drinking sugar-packed cocktails than it does when you're drinking wine, beer, or straight liquor. Once that blood sugar crash comes, you'll be left with far worse cravings than you would have had you of not downed all those sugary drinks. Champagne is also one to avoid here, too. Not only is it healthier to skip out on as much sugar as possible, but it also has the added benefit of lessening your hangovers too!

> **PRO TIP:** *The worst sweet add-ons are sodas, juices, liqueurs, tonic, and bottled drink mixes such as sour mix, daiquiri mix, margarita mix, etc. Steering clear of them can help cut back on calories and sugar.*

Just skip "sour mix" altogether. What is sour mix? It's a sweetened lemon-lime flavored mixer. Common drinks that have it are Amaretto Sour, Whiskey Sour, Tom Collins, Margaritas, and Long Island Iced Teas.

If you can get used to the flavor without it, it's a *great* way to cut calories and sugar. Try omitting it and, instead, squeezing in a few lemons or limes. If you're a margarita fan, go for the "classic" recipe on the rocks, made from only tequila, triple sec, and real lime juice. That alone can potentially save you upwards of a couple hundred calories *per drink* (varies depending on the size of the drink and the brand of sour mix being used).

Use club soda as your mixer. Club soda is not only sugar-free; it's also calorie-free! It won't be sweet like the mixer that you're probably used to, but squeeze in a couple of citrus wedges, and it'll taste much better.

> **PRO TIP:** *Even if you don't go full on with club soda, using it to "cut" your drinks will help cut calories; it will also help you gradually transition over time to just using it as your mixer. So if your thing is usually vodka and Sprite, try out a vodka with half Sprite, half club soda (also known as a "press"). Another popular option is just adding a "splash" of a mixer to give it some added flavor. For example, try out a vodka with club soda and just a splash of cranberry juice!*

If you must use soda, use diet. Yes, there are health concerns raised regarding artificial sweeteners. But, if you want an option that's lower in calories and aren't willing to sacrifice the sweetness, this is one of your only choices. Be careful, though—some studies have shown that you get wasted faster when combining liquor with diet soda!

Skip frozen drinks. These are almost always the highest calorie drinks you can consume. Avoid them at all costs!! These include Piña Coladas, Mudslides, Daiquiris, and Margaritas. In most bars, just choosing a frozen margarita over one on the rocks doubles the calories you'll be taking in.

Skip eating salty snacks. These include nuts, chips, and pretzels. Bars provide these because they make you thirstier, leading you to buy more drinks.

If you know you're prone to snacking, pack a small healthy snack to take with you on your evening binge. It's not okay to eat food you brought into a bar, but you *can* snack on it when walking between bars.

Avoid eating "bad" food the following morning. Typically this is the second exception healthy eaters make to their usually strict diet, and it's a bad one. I know, a big greasy meal after a long night of drinking DOES feel good. You crave that kind of food because your body is yearning for the richest energy source it can find to rectify the effects of all the booze from the night before. This just happens to be fat.

You can prevent this from happening a few different ways. The first big one is to stay hydrated. The next thing experts suggest doing to help is to have a small snack that's high in protein and fiber right before going to bed. Some fiber bars, oatmeal, black beans, whole-wheat pasta, and cereal that are high in fiber are all great suggestions. Combine any of those with at least twenty ounces of water right before you pass out for the night and you should be feeling fine come morning.

Okay, so that's all the harping I'm going to do over keeping your health and body in mind while you're out drinking. Hopefully, you took some good tips away from this section. If you did, I assure you "the older you" will thank you later!

CHAPTER 8:

OH GOD, THE HANGOVER!

Soooo....you didn't take my advice, and now you're left with a brutal hangover. It sucks, doesn't it?!

If this is you, here are a few things you can do to help ease the pain:

Have some water. And then have some more. Water is essential to curing a hangover. Alcohol is a diuretic that can cause massive dehydration. You should have at least crushed out a full 20-ounce glass before you passed out the night before. If you didn't, start catching up now. There's no need to waste your money on expensive sports drinks, either. Research has shown that drinks like Powerade and Gatorade are no better for curing a hangover than water that's straight from your tap.

Pop a multivitamin. It's not a cure, but it may help. Get something that includes lots of B12 and folate.

If nausea is an issue for you, try some bitters and ginger ale. I swear by Angostura bitters. Mix that up with some ginger ale (or even Sprite if you have it) over ice, and it's divine. Some also get great results sipping on ginger tea.

Pop some pain meds. Aspirin, Naproxen, and ibuprofen are all highly recommended. *NEVER* take *anything* with acetaminophen in it. This includes Tylenol, Dayquil/Nyquil, Excedrin, Goody's Powder, Midol, Oxycodone, Percocet, Tramadol, Vicodin, etc. When acetaminophen is combined with a liver that's already working overtime to metabolize all the booze you've consumed, it can cause *severe* liver damage and even death. This isn't even just limited to not taking it while you're hungover, don't *ever* take acetaminophen at *any point* while you're drinking.

Crack a window, or better yet, go for a walk. Studies have shown that oxygen increases the rate that alcohol toxins are broken down in your body, so getting some fresh air is essential. If you're feeling up to it, a walk can be even better as a little exercise will cause your body to release some endorphins which can help boost your mood!

"The hair of the dog." If you're not aware, this is a slang term that means having some more alcohol in the morning in hopes it'll lessen your hangover. There's no conclusive determination of its effectiveness—it works for some and not for others. Some researchers say that all it does is prolong the effects you'll eventually feel from the hangover. Try it at your own risk but be warned: doctors have suggested that your risk of alcohol abuse increases and could lead to alcohol dependency when using this "miracle cure."

Coffee isn't for everyone. For some people caffeine can treat their headaches, for others, it can actually *cause* headaches or make existing ones worse. There are also quite a few studies out there that suggest caffeine can cause dehydration—and since we've already covered that dehydration is a huge part of why you're already feeling like shit, it's not hard to see how MORE dehydration could make you feel even worse than you already do.

Get some carbs in you. These can help with getting your blood sugar levels back up to normal after a long night of drinking, which will, in turn, make you feel less tired and irritable. English muffins, rolls, toast, oatmeal, pancakes, crackers, and plain donuts are all great options here. Pair any of those with a nice glass of fresh fruit juice (avoid OJ due to its acidity) in the morning, and you'll be well on your way to feeling better.

Add some potassium in there too. Spinach and bananas are awesome for this, as is Pedialyte! It's always a good idea to keep a few bottles waiting in your pantry if you go out drinking pretty often. It has twice the sodium and five times as much potassium in it as the same size bottle of Gatorade does!

And some eggs! Eggs are high in taurine and cysteine. Studies have shown that taurine can help reverse the effects a night of drinking has on your liver, and that cysteine helps break down a headache causing toxin that's produced when your body digests alcohol.

COMBO IT UP FOR MASSIVE RESULTS!
It's easy to put all these together. When you wake up, have a tall glass of water mixed with some Pedialyte, along with two ibuprofen and a multivitamin. Then whip up a scrambled egg omelet with some spinach and a side of toast. Take that down along with a glass of fresh apple juice, then head out for a short walk around your neighborhood. You'll be feeling better in no time!

CHAPTER 9:

SO, YOU RUINED YOUR NIGHT

Okay, so you f*%ked up. It's okay. *It happens.* Let's take a second and talk about how to deal with the fallout if you got kicked out, blacked out, threw up, punched down, or any of the other ways you made an ass of yourself.

I'm gonna make this chapter simple and tell you that the right way to deal with pretty much *any* bad situation that may have happened as a result of going too hard is to be accountable for what you've done. That is the key here. Let's go over a few scenarios and the correct way to deal with them if they happen to you.

You got kicked out of a bar. The first step if this happens to you is to find out *why* it happened. Reach out to your friends and *listen* to what they're telling you. If they're all pretty much saying you were in the wrong, then *apologize* for it. Don't make excuses and don't be in denial. Own up to it and make amends.

You got in a fight. Again, find out why it happened. If you were the aggressor then apologize to your friends. If you realize that what you fought over was something stupid then reach out to the person you fought with and apologize to them too. Be the bigger person here. The next time you're in the bar say sorry to the bouncer, manager, and bartender as well. They'll respect you for having accountability.

If it turns out you were the one that was wrongfully attacked it's *still* worth tossing an apology out to your friends as well as the bar staff. Let *them* be the ones to take the responsibility off of you.

Your car got towed. Get it back a.s.a.p. Don't wait! In these situations fees stack up daily so it's absolutely imperative that you handle any kind of towing situation with the quickness.

You embarrassed yourself in front of friends or someone you're interested in. Own up and apologize. If you said or did something you regret the fastest way to get past your mistake is to make it right as soon as possible. Offer to take them out for lunch or send some flowers or an apology card.

You puked on someone or in their car or house. CLEAN IT UP! If they've already cleaned it up then offer to have their clothing dry cleaned/replaced or their car/house professionally detailed/cleaned. If they say it isn't necessary then at the very least take them out for a meal on you.

If you puked in an Uber you're gonna have to pay the cleaning fee. If it was an Uber your friend paid for then you are *absolutely* responsible for reimbursing them for the fee.

If you puked in your favorite bar then show up the next day and apologize. Find out who had to end up cleaning your mess and slip them a $20 bill while shaking their hand.

You damaged something that didn't belong to you. REPLACE IT! It doesn't matter what it is, if your drunk ass broke it then your sober ass has to buy it.

You woke up and have no idea what happened the night before and/or how you got to where you currently are. Waking up and having no recollection of how you ended up where you are can be *terrifying*. If you find yourself in this situation it's important to first identify where you are and who you're with. If you're at home or a friends house, great! If you don't recognize where you are or who you're with then you have a whole lot to start figuring out.

After establishing where you are find out where your belongings are. Do you have your phone? Keys? Car? Wallet? Purse? Credit Card? Reach out to the people you were out with the night before and ask questions so you can piece together exactly what happened.

In the vast majority of these situations you'll mostly likely end up finding out that someone had to take care of you for the night. They probably paid your bar tab for you and maybe even covered the cost of your transportation home. This friend is THE SHIT and needs to be thanked accordingly. Not only did they cover the financial side of things for you, they more than likely also sacrificed their entire night of fun in exchange for babysitting your drunk ass. Pay up any and all money they covered for you *immediately* and take this person out for a nice dinner and let them know how much you appreciate them for looking out for you.

LEARN FROM IT AND DON'T LET IT HAPPEN AGAIN.

This is the big one. Every person that's new to drinking makes mistakes and has "that one night." Keyword here being *one*. People are by nature very forgiving. When I think about every friend or acquaintance I have they *all* have a story or two about a night that spiraled out of control. Just don't make it a habit. Your friends will more than likely look past one or two off nights but when you keep doing it over and over again you'll quickly find out that less and less people will want to go out with you. You'll begin to develop a reputation as *that* drunk, and trust me when I say that you do not want that. I see so many of these types in my line of work and I watch as it just gets worse and worse each time it happens. Their real friends aren't there anymore, they're out with a new group of people every single time, and their antics just look more and more pathetic as they continue to get older. More often than not this is also the same person that "can't find a good relationship," starts packing on weight, and starts stacking up DUI's. Believe me when I tell you that it's a slippery slope to be on if you can't reign in that kind of behavior.

CHAPTER 10:

LAST CALL!

You made it to the end. CONGRATULATIONS! You now have all the essential tools you need to be a master of the bar. Before we wrap up, let's take a look back at the picture I painted for you at the very beginning of this book:

It's a Saturday night, and the bar is packed six people deep. Everyone's smooshed in trying to get their light beer and shot of Fireball and, by all accounts, failing miserably at doing so. All of a sudden, and with little fanfare, drinks are produced and passed over the top of the huge mass of thirsty zombies alllllll the way in the back to YOU.

With that, my job is done here. I wish you the best of luck out there on the bar scene. Be respectful, be kind, be courteous, and most importantly, be *safe*.

Made in the USA
San Bernardino, CA
17 April 2020